SCIENCE COMICS

ROCKETS

Defying Gravity

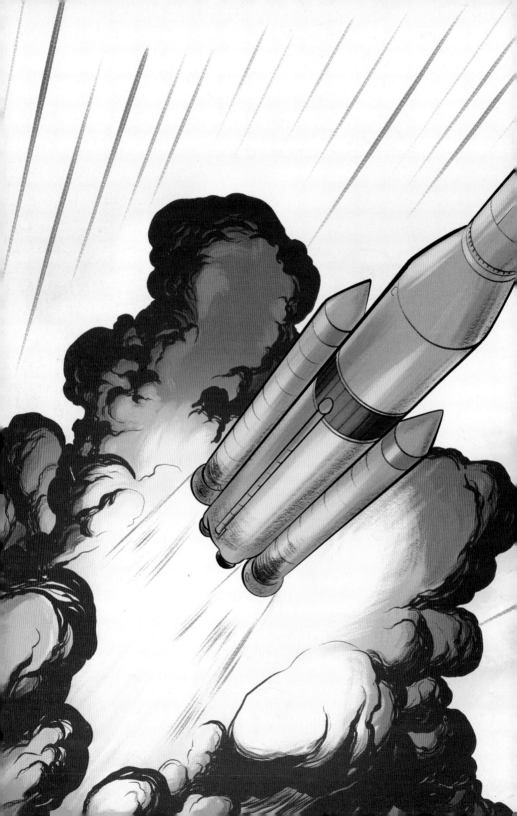

ROCKETS
Defying Gravity

Anne Drozd
Jerzy Drozd

:01
First Second
New York

For all of the animals who helped humans
take rockets to the skies and beyond.

First Second

Copyright © 2018 by Anne Drozd and Jerzy Drozd

Penciled with a Pentel Twist-Erase pencil and Clip Studio Paint. Inked with a Kuretake G-Pen nib on Strathmore 300 Series smooth Bristol, as well as self-made digital brushes in Clip Studio Paint. Colored digitally in Clip Studio Paint and lettered in Adobe Illustrator.

Published by First Second
First Second is an imprint of Roaring Brook Press,
a division of Holtzbrinck Publishing Holdings Limited Partnership
175 Fifth Avenue, New York, NY 10010
All rights reserved

Library of Congress Congress Control Number: 2017946155

Paperback ISBN: 978-1-62672-825-7
Hardcover ISBN: 978-1-62672-826-4

Our books may be purchased in bulk for promotional, educational, or business use. Please contact your local bookseller or the Macmillan Corporate and Premium Sales Department at (800) 221-7945 ext. 5442 or by e-mail at MacmillanSpecialMarkets@macmillan.com.

First edition 2018
Edited by Dave Roman
Book design by John Green
Physics consultant: David Coupland

Printed in China by Toppan Leefung Printing Ltd., Dongguan City, Guangdong Province
Paperback: 10 9 8 7 6 5 4 3 2 1
Hardcover: 10 9 8 7 6 5 4 3 2 1

Ten. Nine. Eight. Seven . . .

Inside your head, you're already counting the rest of the way down, aren't you?

Three. Two. One. LIFTOFF!

A blinding flare of light. An intense roar. An enormous column of engineering slooooowwwwly begins to rise upward, speeding up, faster, faster. You crane your neck and try not to blink as the spacecraft disappears from sight, leaving an arc of white smoke behind. Maybe you wish you were on the rocket.

Rockets are scary. They contain huge amounts of incredibly explosive chemicals. On top of them, we put spacecraft that cost hundreds of millions of dollars. Sometimes we even put people up there. And then we light the rocket and hope for the best. Rocket scientists have a saying: a thousand things can happen during a rocket launch, and only one of them is good.

Despite how powerful and dangerous they are, rockets today are very reliable. Rockets have launched humans to the Moon, and could send people to Mars or asteroids soon. Robots have traveled farther. Inward to Venus and Mercury. Outward to Mars and the giant planets. Robots have landed on Mars and on Saturn's giant moon Titan and on

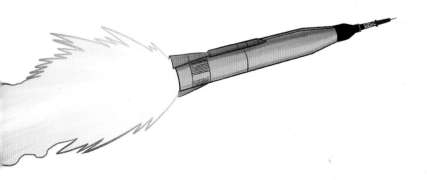

a comet named Churyumov-Gerasimenko. If you could launch a robot on a rocket, where would you explore?

Space explorers owe thanks to the pioneers of rocketry, and to the people who continue to make rockets lighter, more efficient, more reliable, more precise, and cheaper. You'll learn about some of them in this book.

When humans first started developing modern science and technology, scientists and engineers worked mostly alone, or in small groups. In a book like this one, we can name those original individuals—Isaac Newton, Claude Ruggieri, Qian Xuesen—but the more modern and complex science gets, the more people are involved; it's impossible to name all of them. That's a good thing, if you like space exploration, because there are more ways than ever to get involved.

When we send an astronaut or a robot into space, it's never just one astronaut or robot doing the exploring. It takes thousands of people working in all kinds of roles to make a space mission a success. And they're not all genius inventors.

Do you like math and physics? You can be a rocket designer or an astronomer. Do you like chemistry and making things? You could

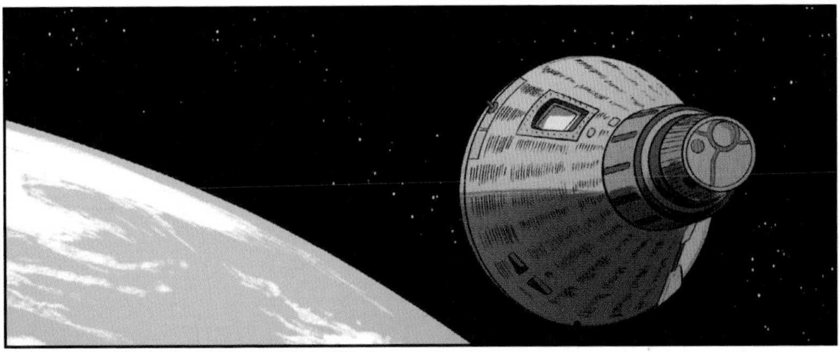

develop rocket fuel or study the minerals of other worlds. Do you like to code? You could write software for rockets or for driving robots on Mars. Are you the kind of person who worries about what will happen if something goes wrong on a rocket? There are jobs checking the work of the engineers to make sure they have made no mistakes. Do you like to take charge of group projects? All those scientists, engineers, and programmers work in teams that need to be coordinated to get big projects done. Do you like to write, tell stories, or create art? Space missions need educators, storytellers, technical writers, and press officers to explain to the world how all of this works.

When a robot sends pictures from Mars or Saturn and you look at them on your computer, you are part of that mission, exploring space through the robot's eyes. If you ask even one question, you're beginning to do science.

I hope you'll enjoy this introduction to rocketry, and that someday—whether you do it through a robot's eyes, or atop your own rocket—you get to explore space.

—Emily Lakdawalla,
planetary geologist, science writer,
and senior editor at the Planetary Society

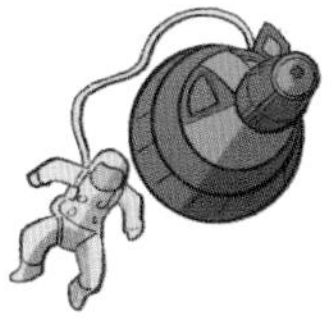

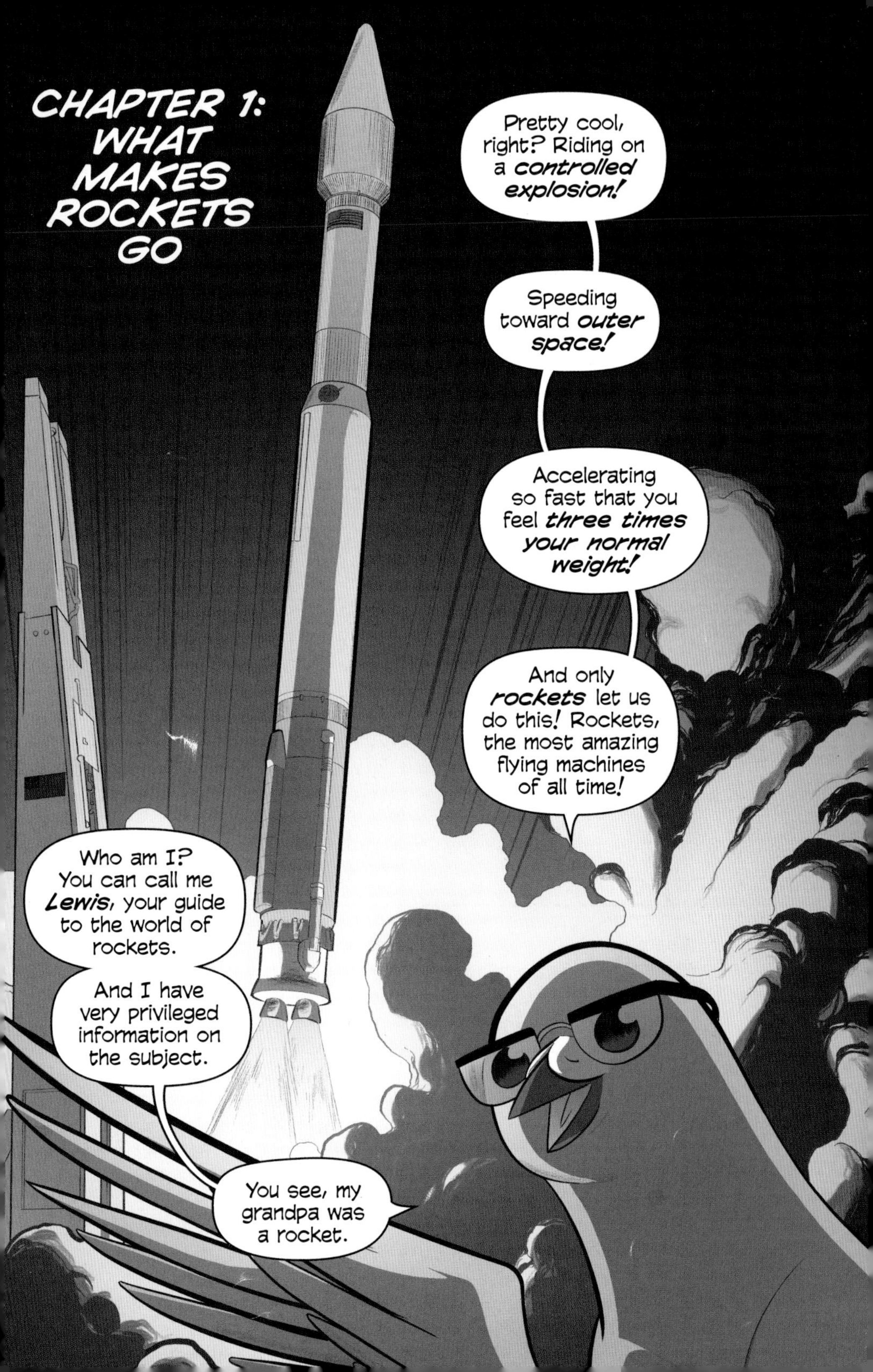
CHAPTER 1: WHAT MAKES ROCKETS GO
Pretty cool, right? Riding on a controlled explosion!
Speeding toward outer space!
Accelerating so fast that you feel three times your normal weight!
And only rockets let us do this! Rockets, the most amazing flying machines of all time!
Who am I? You can call me Lewis, your guide to the world of rockets.
And I have very privileged information on the subject.
You see, my grandpa was a rocket.

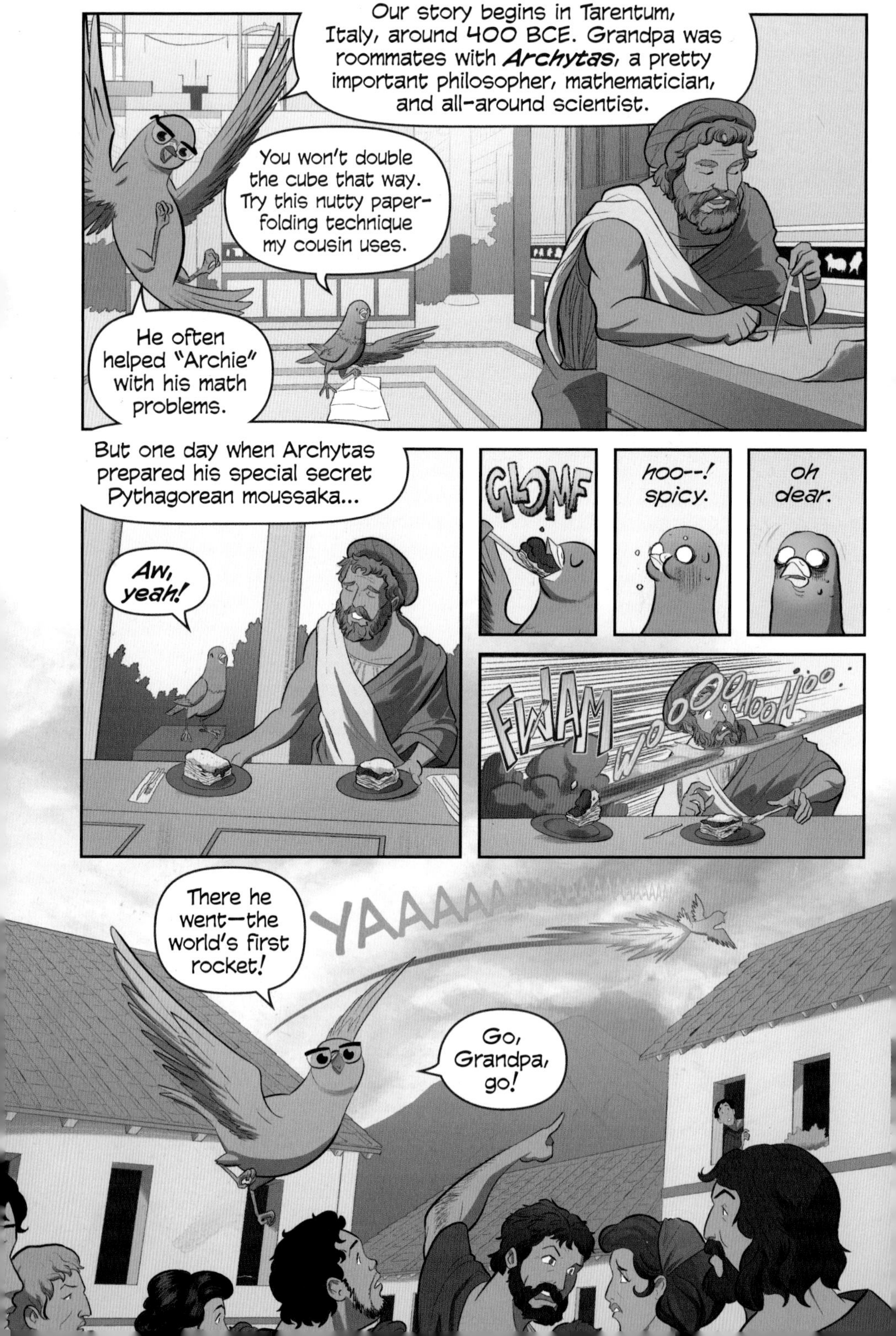
Our story begins in Tarentum, Italy, around 400 BCE. Grandpa was roommates with *Archytas*, a pretty important philosopher, mathematician, and all-around scientist.
You won't double the cube that way. Try this nutty paper-folding technique my cousin uses.
He often helped "Archie" with his math problems.
But one day when Archytas prepared his special secret Pythagorean moussaka...
Aw, yeah!
GLOMF
hoo--! spicy.
oh dear.
FWAM
WOOOOOHOOH
There he went—the world's first rocket!
YAAAA
Go, Grandpa, go!

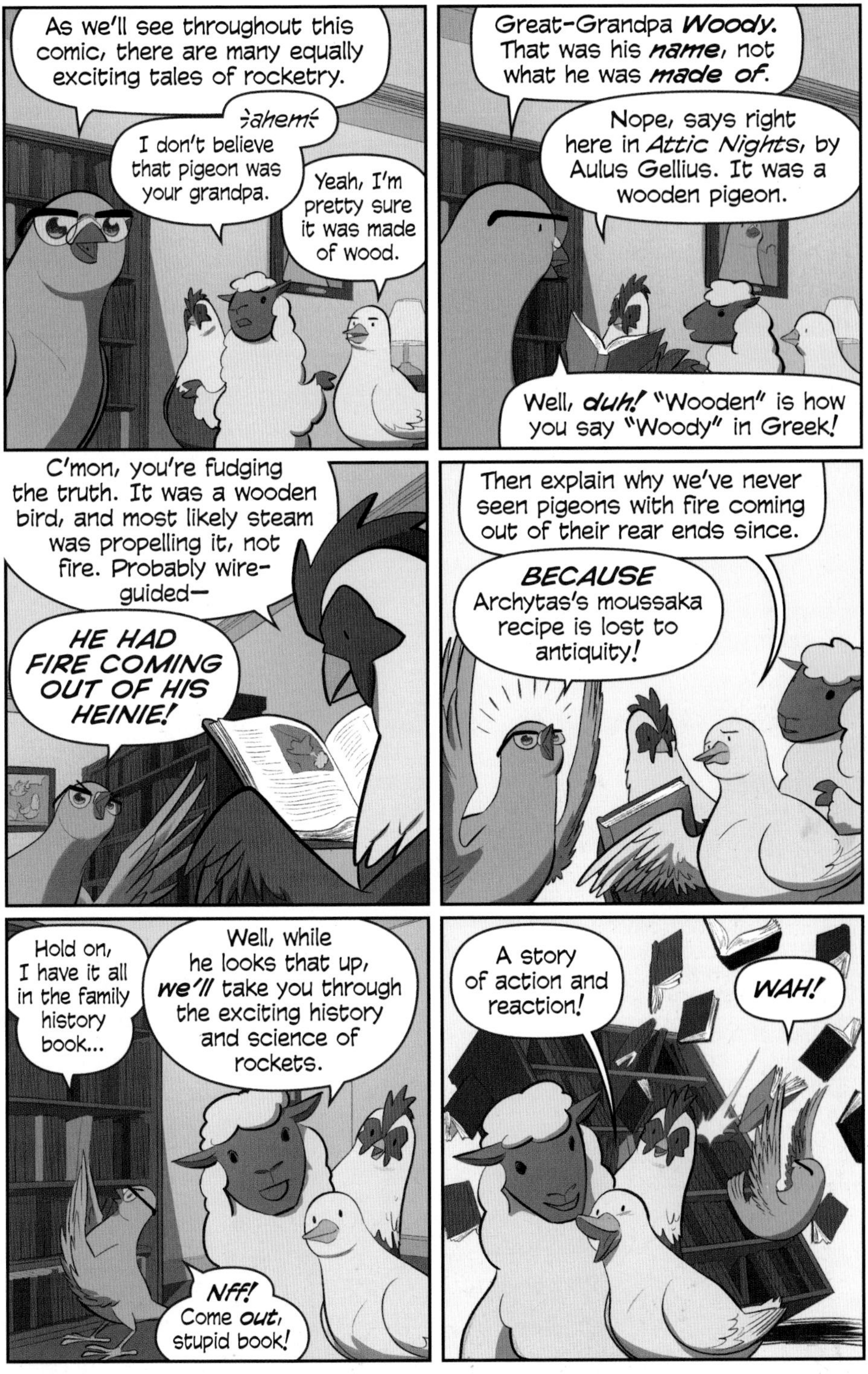
As we'll see throughout this comic, there are many equally exciting tales of rocketry.
ahem I don't believe that pigeon was your grandpa.
Yeah, I'm pretty sure it was made of wood.
Great-Grandpa **Woody.** That was his **name,** not what he was **made of.**
Nope, says right here in *Attic Nights,* by Aulus Gellius. It was a wooden pigeon.
Well, **duh!** "Wooden" is how you say "Woody" in Greek!
C'mon, you're fudging the truth. It was a wooden bird, and most likely steam was propelling it, not fire. Probably wire-guided—
HE HAD FIRE COMING OUT OF HIS HEINIE!
Then explain why we've never seen pigeons with fire coming out of their rear ends since.
BECAUSE Archytas's moussaka recipe is lost to antiquity!
Hold on, I have it all in the family history book...
Well, while he looks that up, **we'll** take you through the exciting history and science of rockets.
Nff! Come **out,** stupid book!
A story of action and reaction!
WAH!

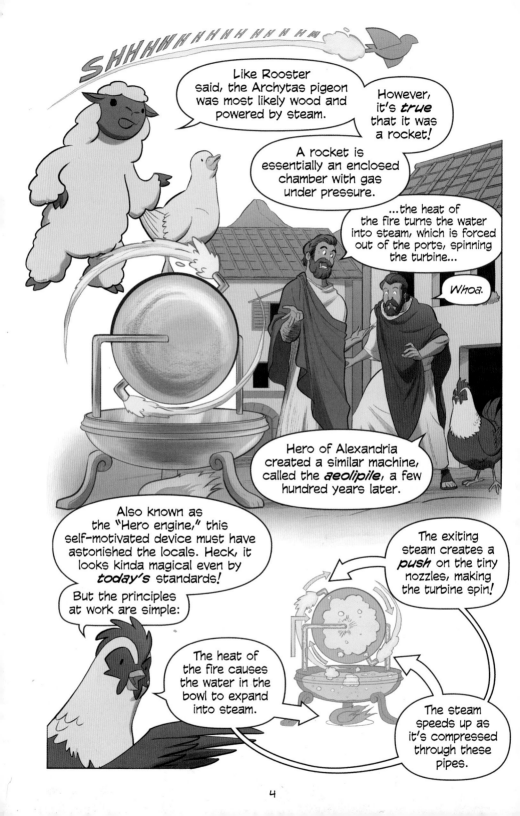

SHHHWHHHHHHHHHM

Like Rooster said, the Archytas pigeon was most likely wood and powered by steam.

However, it's *true* that it was a rocket!

A rocket is essentially an enclosed chamber with gas under pressure.

...the heat of the fire turns the water into steam, which is forced out of the ports, spinning the turbine...

Whoa.

Hero of Alexandria created a similar machine, called the *aeolipile*, a few hundred years later.

Also known as the "Hero engine," this self-motivated device must have astonished the locals. Heck, it looks kinda magical even by *today's* standards!

But the principles at work are simple:

The exiting steam creates a *push* on the tiny nozzles, making the turbine spin!

The heat of the fire causes the water in the bowl to expand into steam.

The steam speeds up as it's compressed through these pipes.

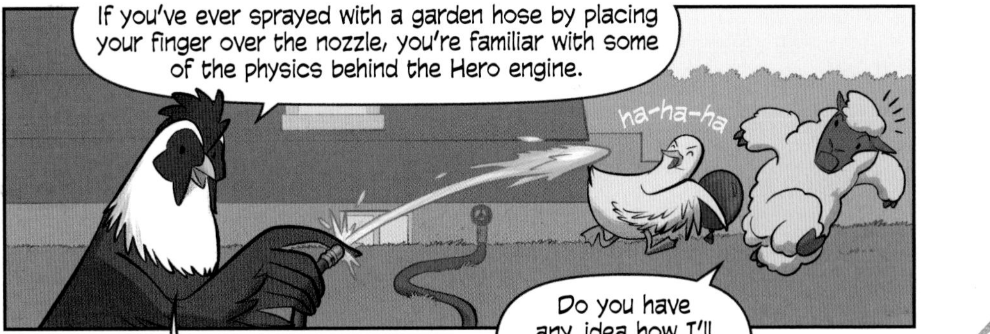
If you've ever sprayed with a garden hose by placing your finger over the nozzle, you're familiar with some of the physics behind the Hero engine.
ha-ha-ha
Do you have any idea how I'll *smell* if you get me with that hose?

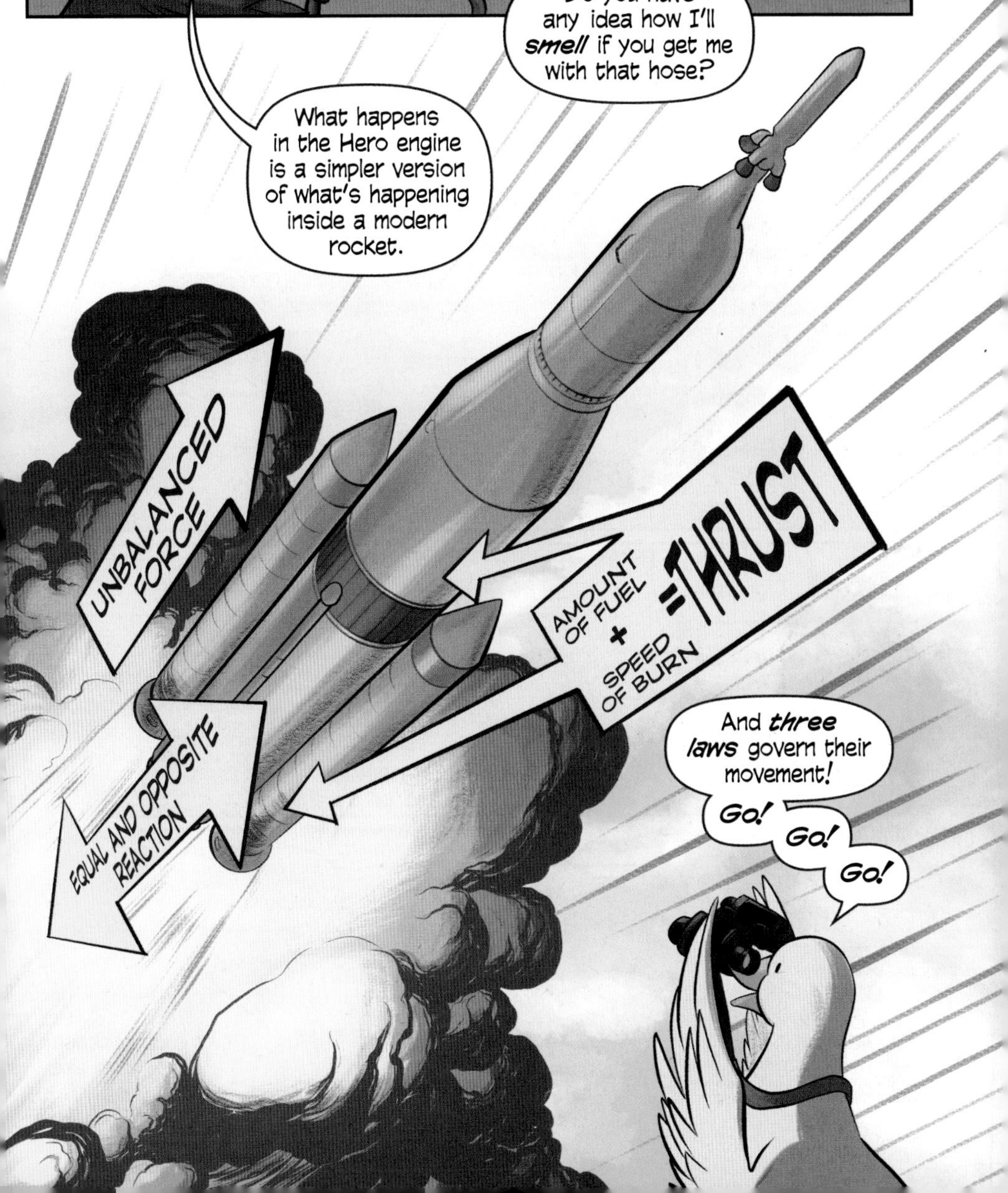
What happens in the Hero engine is a simpler version of what's happening inside a modern rocket.
UNBALANCED FORCE
AMOUNT OF FUEL + SPEED OF BURN =THRUST
EQUAL AND OPPOSITE REACTION
And *three laws* govern their movement!
Go!
Go!
Go!

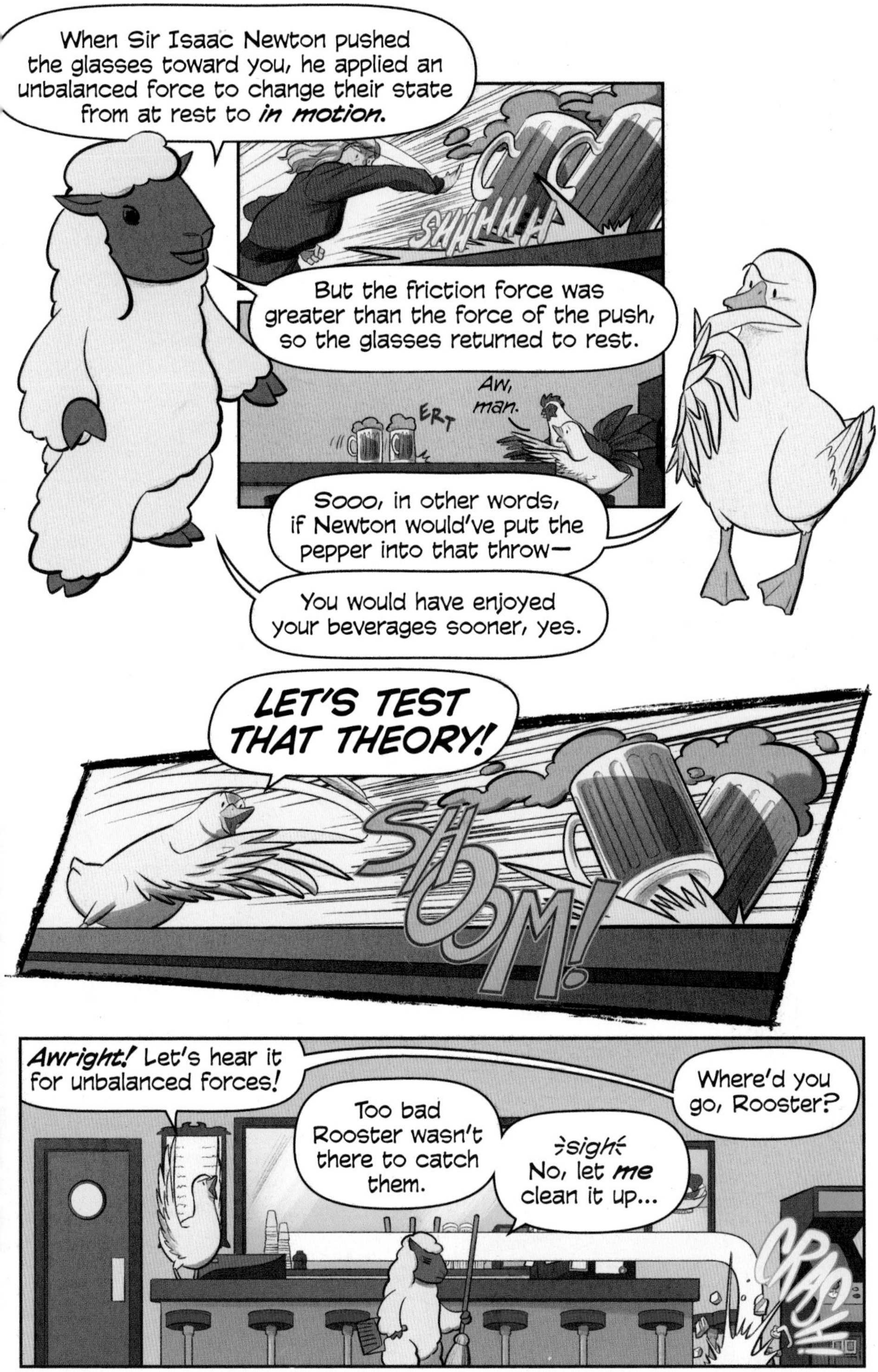
When Sir Isaac Newton pushed the glasses toward you, he applied an unbalanced force to change their state from at rest to *in motion.*
SHHHHH
But the friction force was greater than the force of the push, so the glasses returned to rest.
ERT
Aw, man.
Sooo, in other words, if Newton would've put the pepper into that throw—
You would have enjoyed your beverages sooner, yes.
LET'S TEST THAT THEORY!
SHOOM!
Awright! Let's hear it for unbalanced forces!
Too bad Rooster wasn't there to catch them.
Where'd you go, Rooster?
sigh
No, let *me* clean it up...
CRASH!

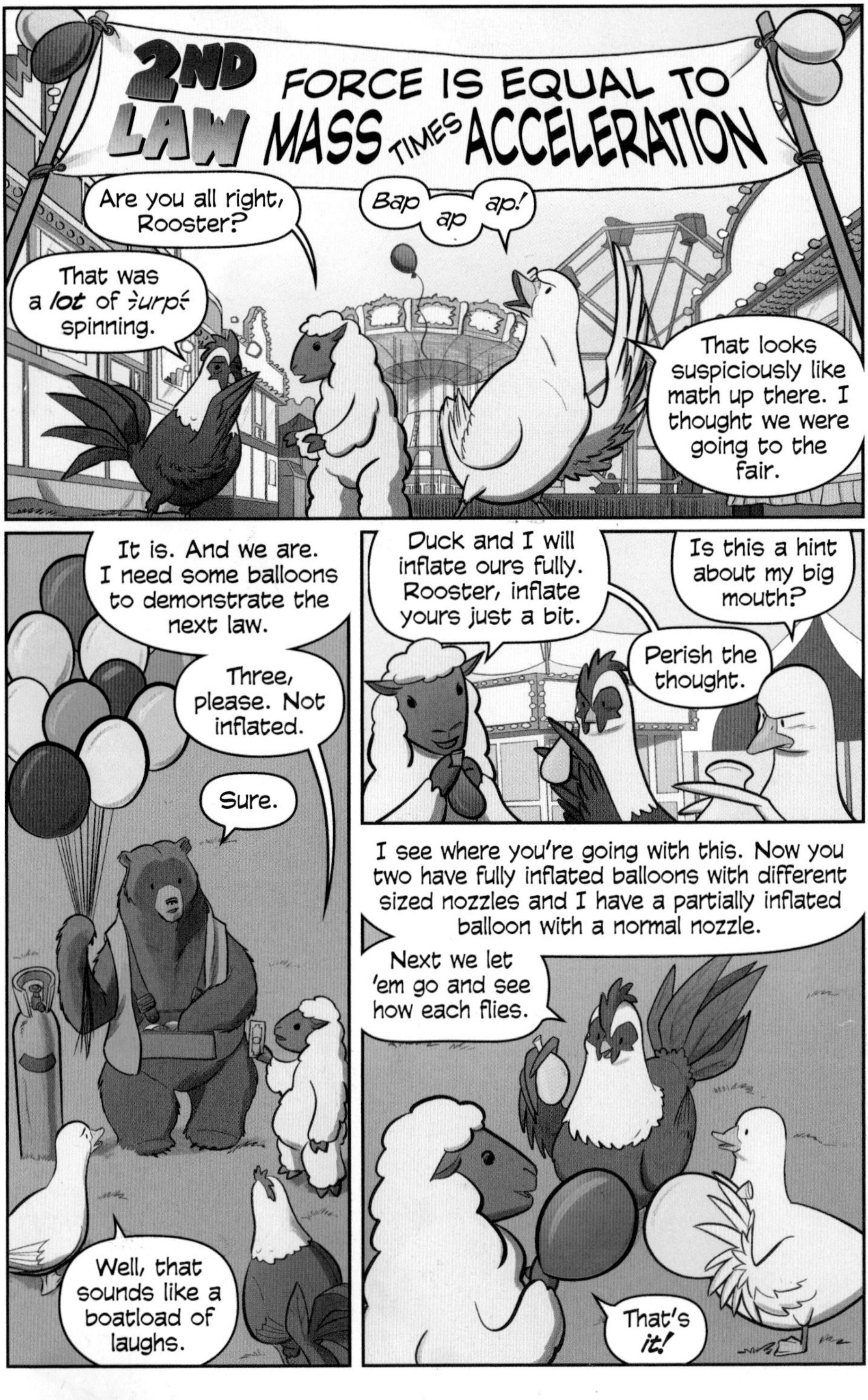
2ND LAW
FORCE IS EQUAL TO MASS TIMES ACCELERATION
Are you all right, Rooster?
Bap ap ap!
That was a *lot* of *urp* spinning.
That looks suspiciously like math up there. I thought we were going to the fair.
It is. And we are. I need some balloons to demonstrate the next law.
Three, please. Not inflated.
Sure.
Well, that sounds like a boatload of laughs.
Duck and I will inflate ours fully. Rooster, inflate yours just a bit.
Is this a hint about my big mouth?
Perish the thought.
I see where you're going with this. Now you two have fully inflated balloons with different sized nozzles and I have a partially inflated balloon with a normal nozzle.
Next we let 'em go and see how each flies.
That's *it!*

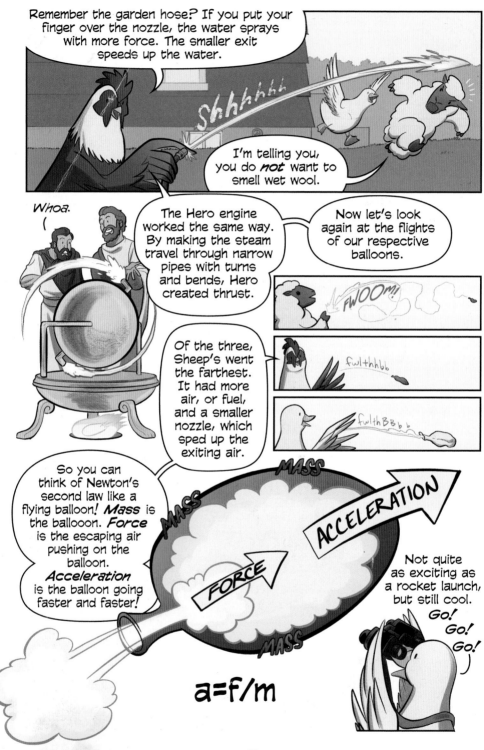

Remember the garden hose? If you put your finger over the nozzle, the water sprays with more force. The smaller exit speeds up the water.

Shhhhhh

I'm telling you, you do *not* want to smell wet wool.

Whoa.

The Hero engine worked the same way. By making the steam travel through narrow pipes with turns and bends, Hero created thrust.

Now let's look again at the flights of our respective balloons.

FWOOM!

Of the three, Sheep's went the farthest. It had more air, or fuel, and a smaller nozzle, which sped up the exiting air.

fwlthhbb

fwlthBBbb

So you can think of Newton's second law like a flying balloon! *Mass* is the balloon. *Force* is the escaping air pushing on the balloon. *Acceleration* is the balloon going faster and faster!

MASS

MASS

ACCELERATION

FORCE

MASS

Not quite as exciting as a rocket launch, but still cool.

Go!
Go!
Go!

a=f/m

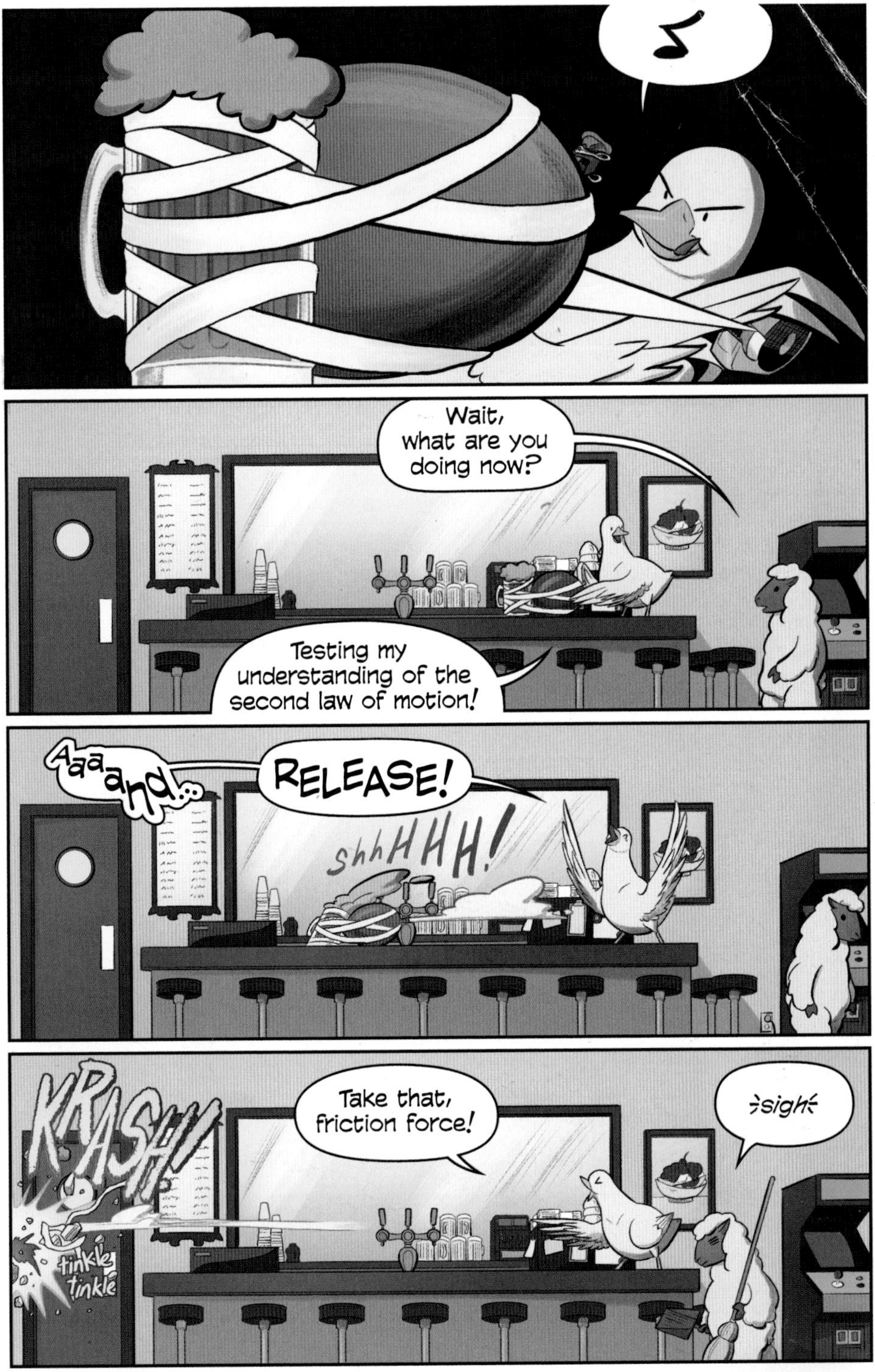
Wait, what are you doing now?
Testing my understanding of the second law of motion!
Aaaand...
RELEASE!
shhHHHH!
KRASH!
tinkle tinkle
Take that, friction force!
sigh

19

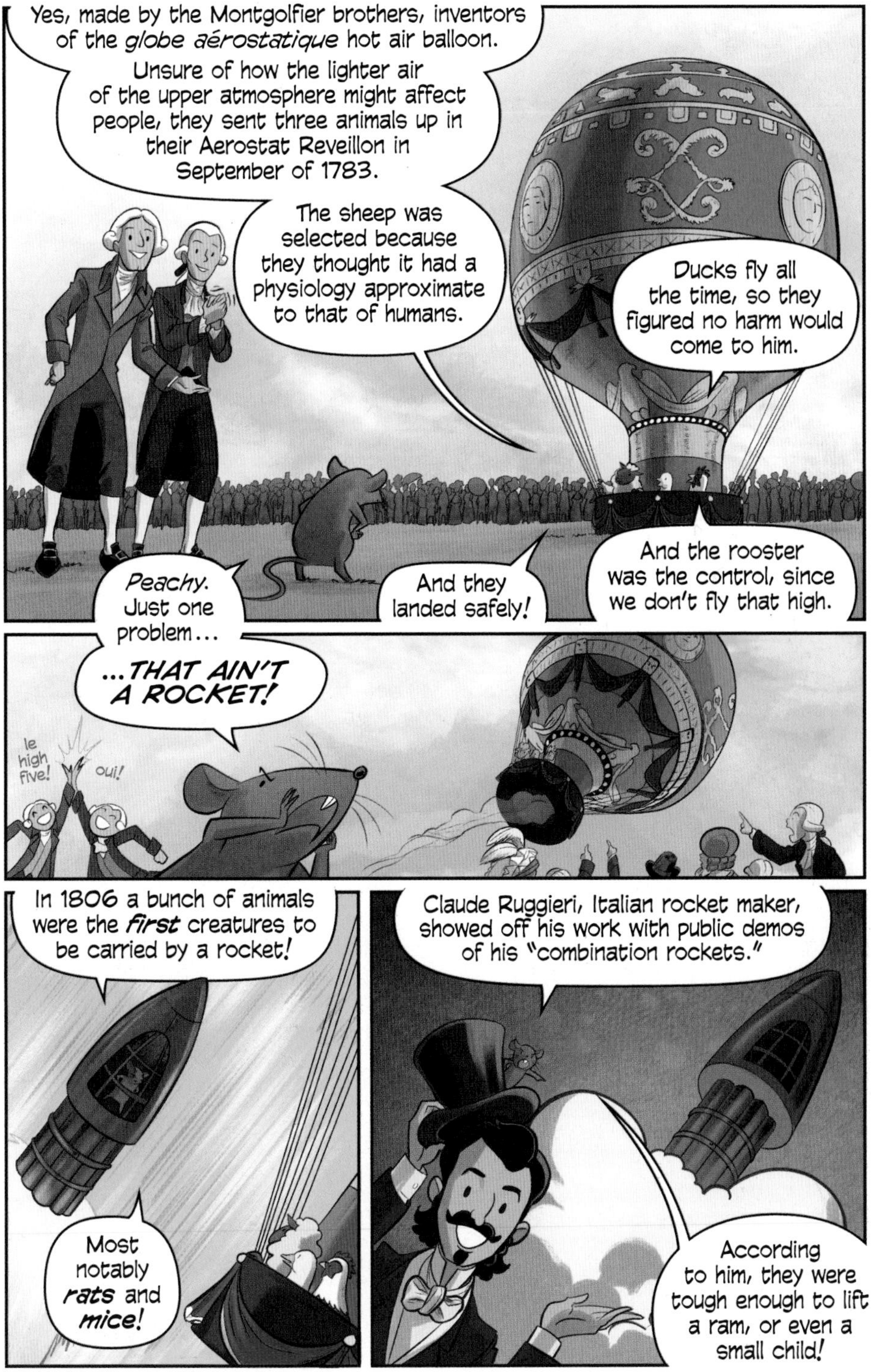
Yes, made by the Montgolfier brothers, inventors of the *globe aérostatique* hot air balloon.
Unsure of how the lighter air of the upper atmosphere might affect people, they sent three animals up in their Aerostat Reveillon in September of 1783.
The sheep was selected because they thought it had a physiology approximate to that of humans.
Ducks fly all the time, so they figured no harm would come to him.
And the rooster was the control, since we don't fly that high.
And they landed safely!
Peachy. Just one problem...
...THAT AIN'T A ROCKET!
le high five!
oui!
In 1806 a bunch of animals were the *first* creatures to be carried by a rocket!
Most notably *rats* and *mice*!
Claude Ruggieri, Italian rocket maker, showed off his work with public demos of his "combination rockets."
According to him, they were tough enough to lift a ram, or even a small child!

CHAPTER 2: ROCKETS AS ENTERTAINMENT

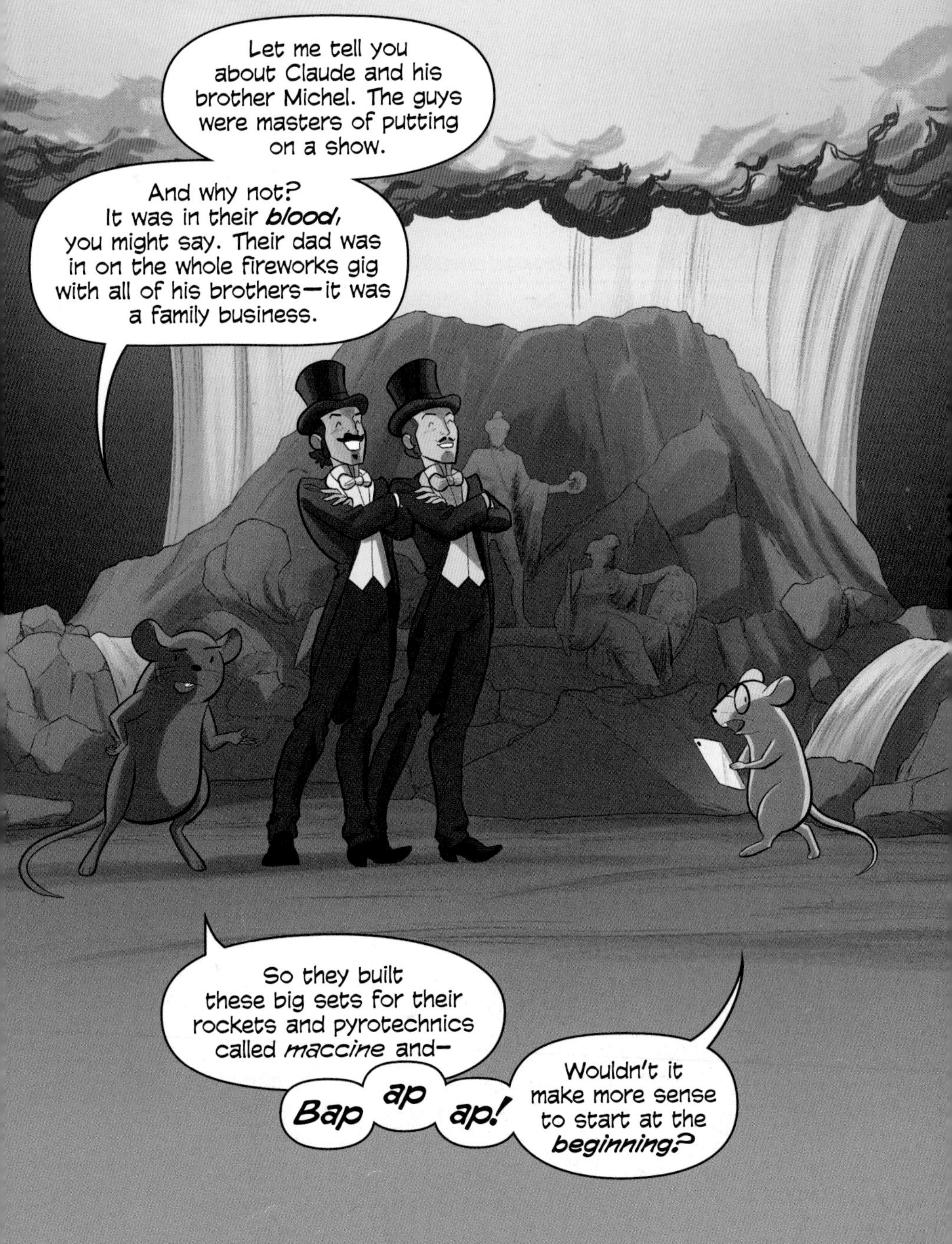

Let me tell you about Claude and his brother Michel. The guys were masters of putting on a show.
And why not? It was in their *blood*, you might say. Their dad was in on the whole fireworks gig with all of his brothers—it was a family business.
So they built these big sets for their rockets and pyrotechnics called *maccine* and—
Bap ap ap!
Wouldn't it make more sense to start at the *beginning?*

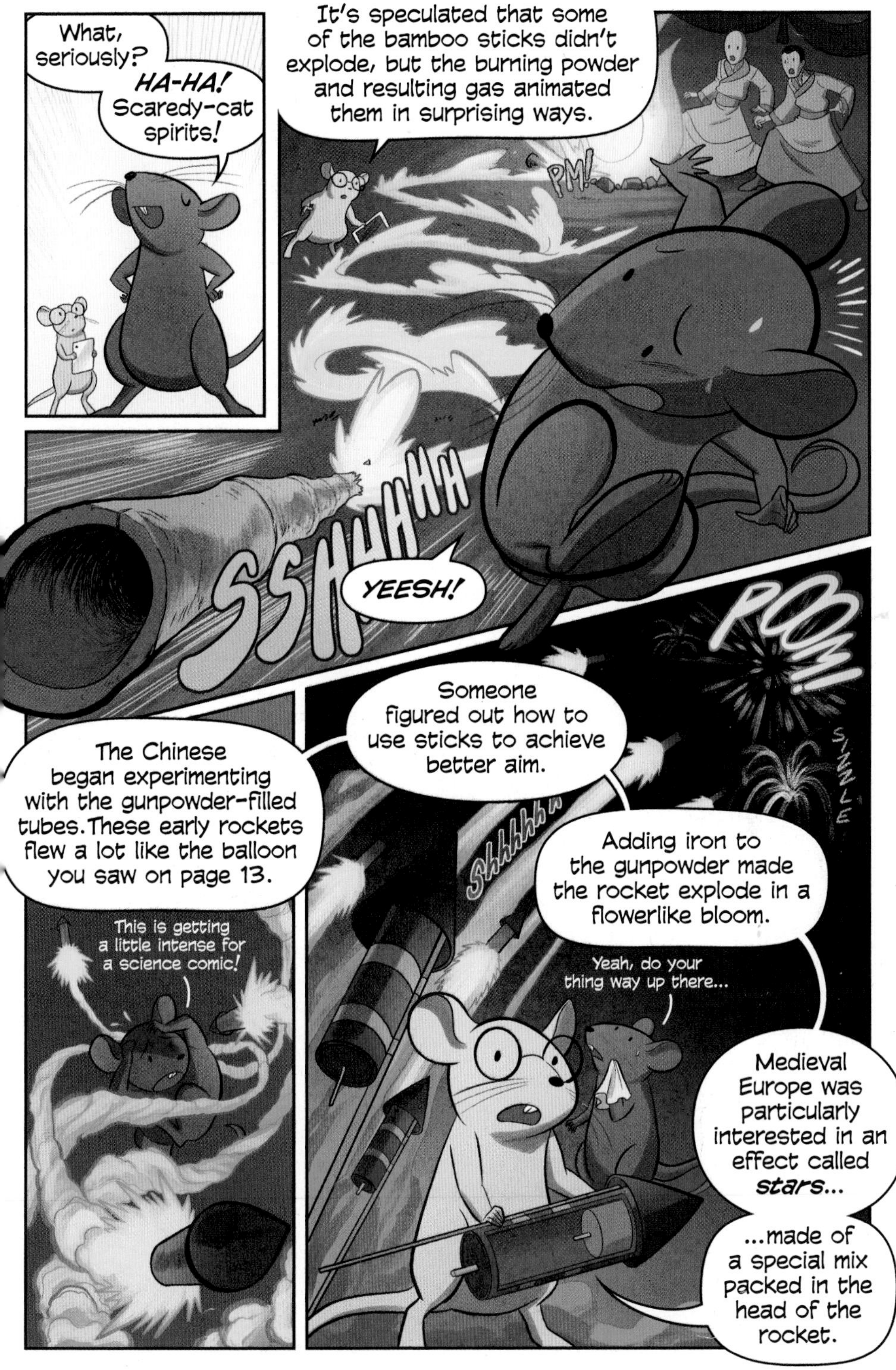

What, seriously?
HA-HA! Scaredy-cat spirits!
It's speculated that some of the bamboo sticks didn't explode, but the burning powder and resulting gas animated them in surprising ways.
PM!
SSHHHHHH
YEESH!
POOM!!
SIZZLE
The Chinese began experimenting with the gunpowder-filled tubes. These early rockets flew a lot like the balloon you saw on page 13.
This is getting a little intense for a science comic!
Someone figured out how to use sticks to achieve better aim.
Shhhhhh
Adding iron to the gunpowder made the rocket explode in a flowerlike bloom.
Yeah, do your thing way up there...
Medieval Europe was particularly interested in an effect called ***stars***...
...made of a special mix packed in the head of the rocket.

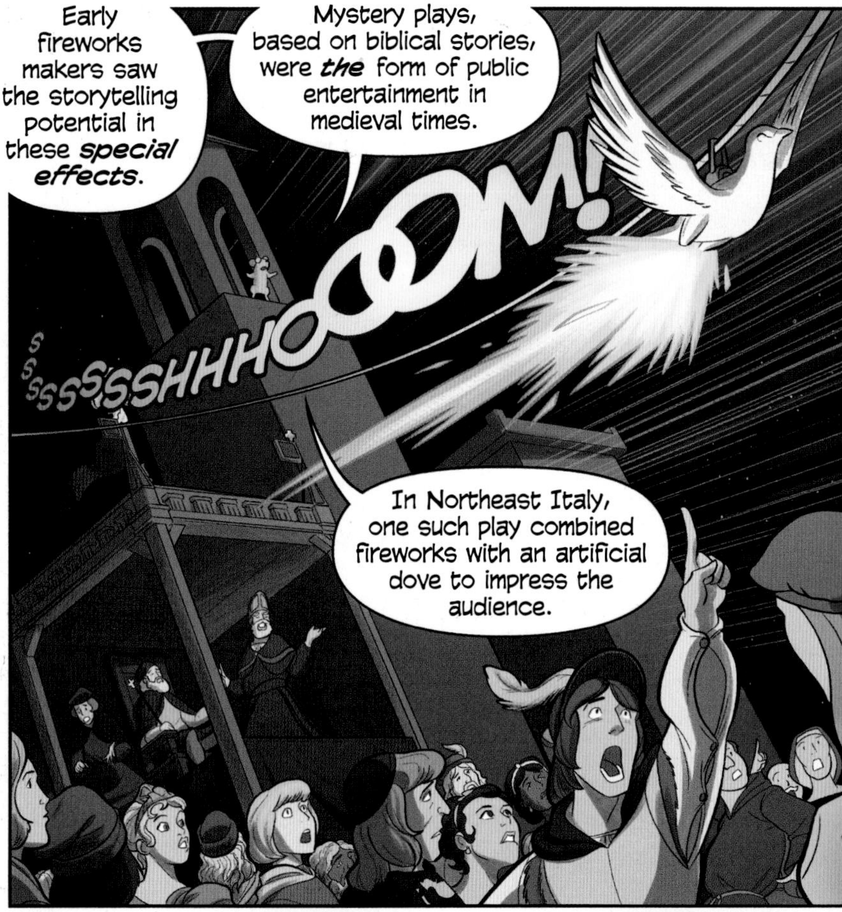
Early fireworks makers saw the storytelling potential in these *special effects*.
Mystery plays, based on biblical stories, were *the* form of public entertainment in medieval times.
SSSSSSSHHHOOOOM!
In Northeast Italy, one such play combined fireworks with an artificial dove to impress the audience.

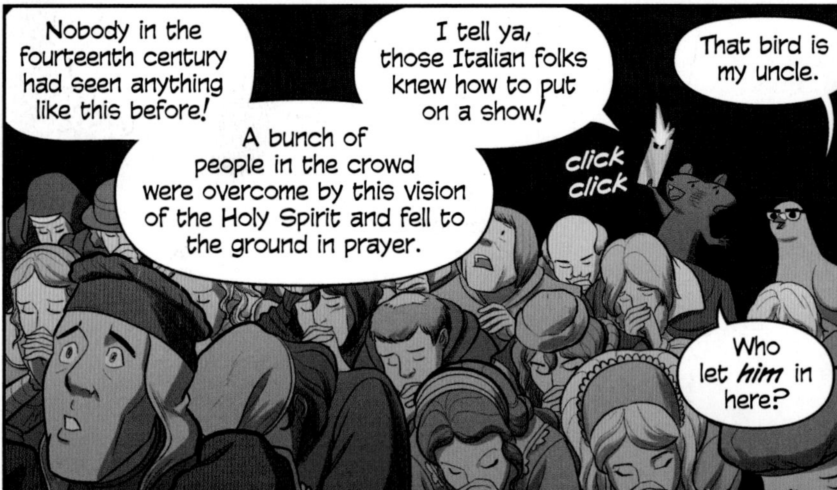
Nobody in the fourteenth century had seen anything like this before!
A bunch of people in the crowd were overcome by this vision of the Holy Spirit and fell to the ground in prayer.
I tell ya, those Italian folks knew how to put on a show!
click click
That bird is my uncle.
Who let *him* in here?

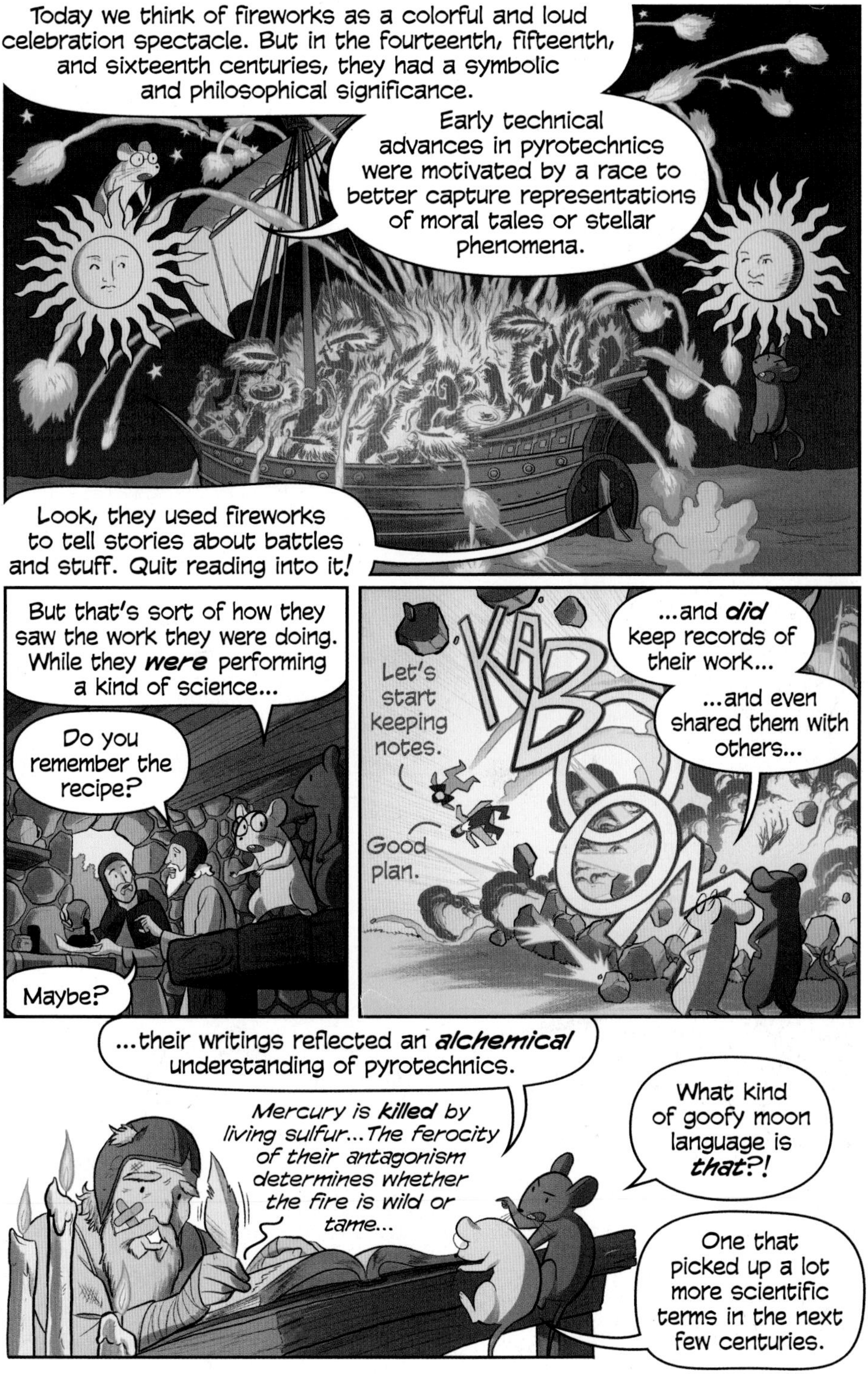
Today we think of fireworks as a colorful and loud celebration spectacle. But in the fourteenth, fifteenth, and sixteenth centuries, they had a symbolic and philosophical significance.
Early technical advances in pyrotechnics were motivated by a race to better capture representations of moral tales or stellar phenomena.
Look, they used fireworks to tell stories about battles and stuff. Quit reading into it!
But that's sort of how they saw the work they were doing. While they *were* performing a kind of science...
Do you remember the recipe?
Maybe?
Let's start keeping notes.
Good plan.
KABOOM
...and *did* keep records of their work...
...and even shared them with others...
...their writings reflected an *alchemical* understanding of pyrotechnics.
Mercury is ***killed*** *by living sulfur...The ferocity of their antagonism determines whether the fire is wild or tame...*
What kind of goofy moon language is ***that***?!
One that picked up a lot more scientific terms in the next few centuries.

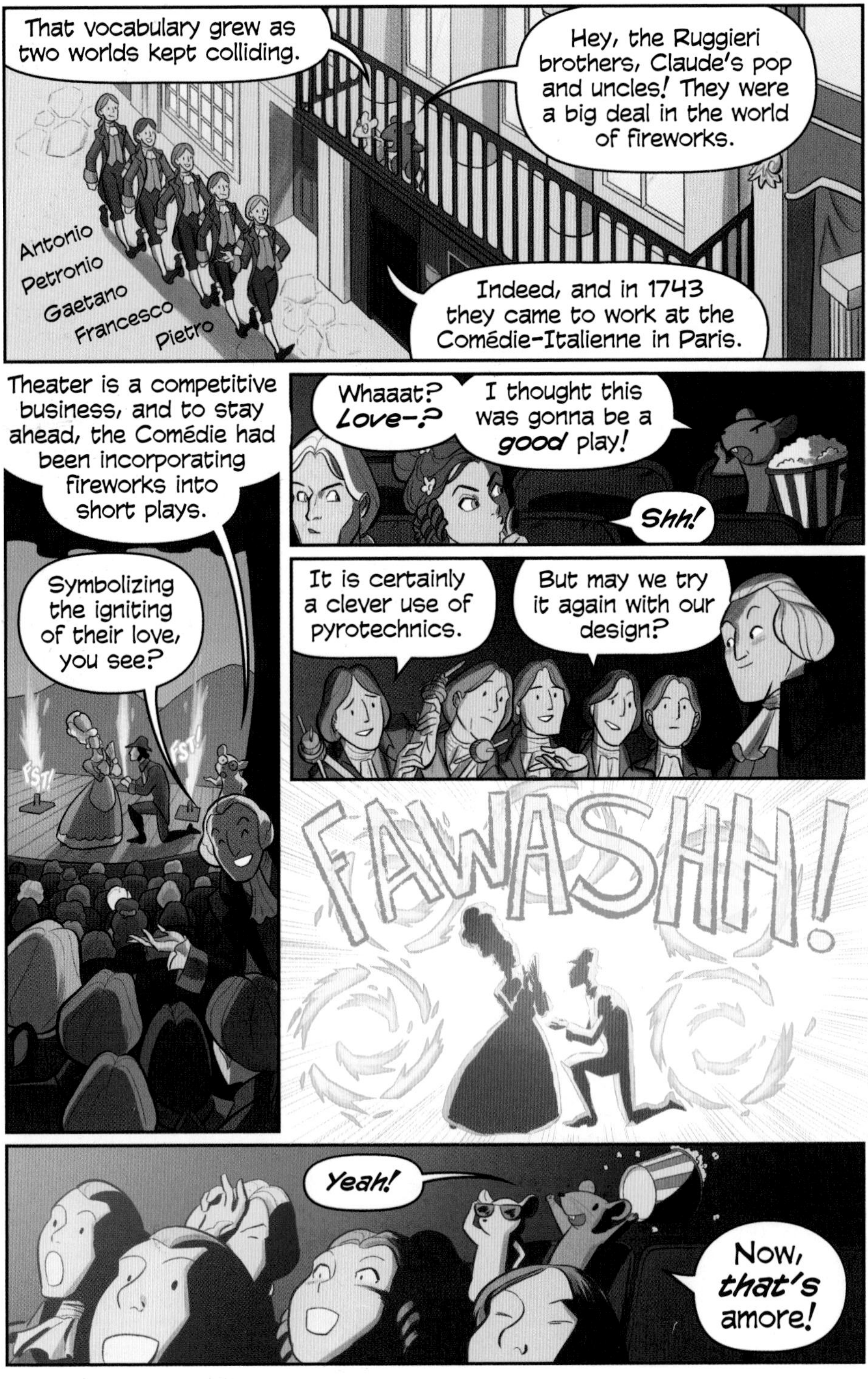

That vocabulary grew as two worlds kept colliding.
Hey, the Ruggieri brothers, Claude's pop and uncles! They were a big deal in the world of fireworks.
Antonio
Petronio
Gaetano
Francesco
Pietro
Indeed, and in 1743 they came to work at the Comédie-Italienne in Paris.
Theater is a competitive business, and to stay ahead, the Comédie had been incorporating fireworks into short plays.
Symbolizing the igniting of their love, you see?
FST!
FST!
Whaaat? *Love-?*
I thought this was gonna be a *good* play!
Shh!
It is certainly a clever use of pyrotechnics.
But may we try it again with our design?
FAWASHH!
Yeah!
Now, *that's* amore!

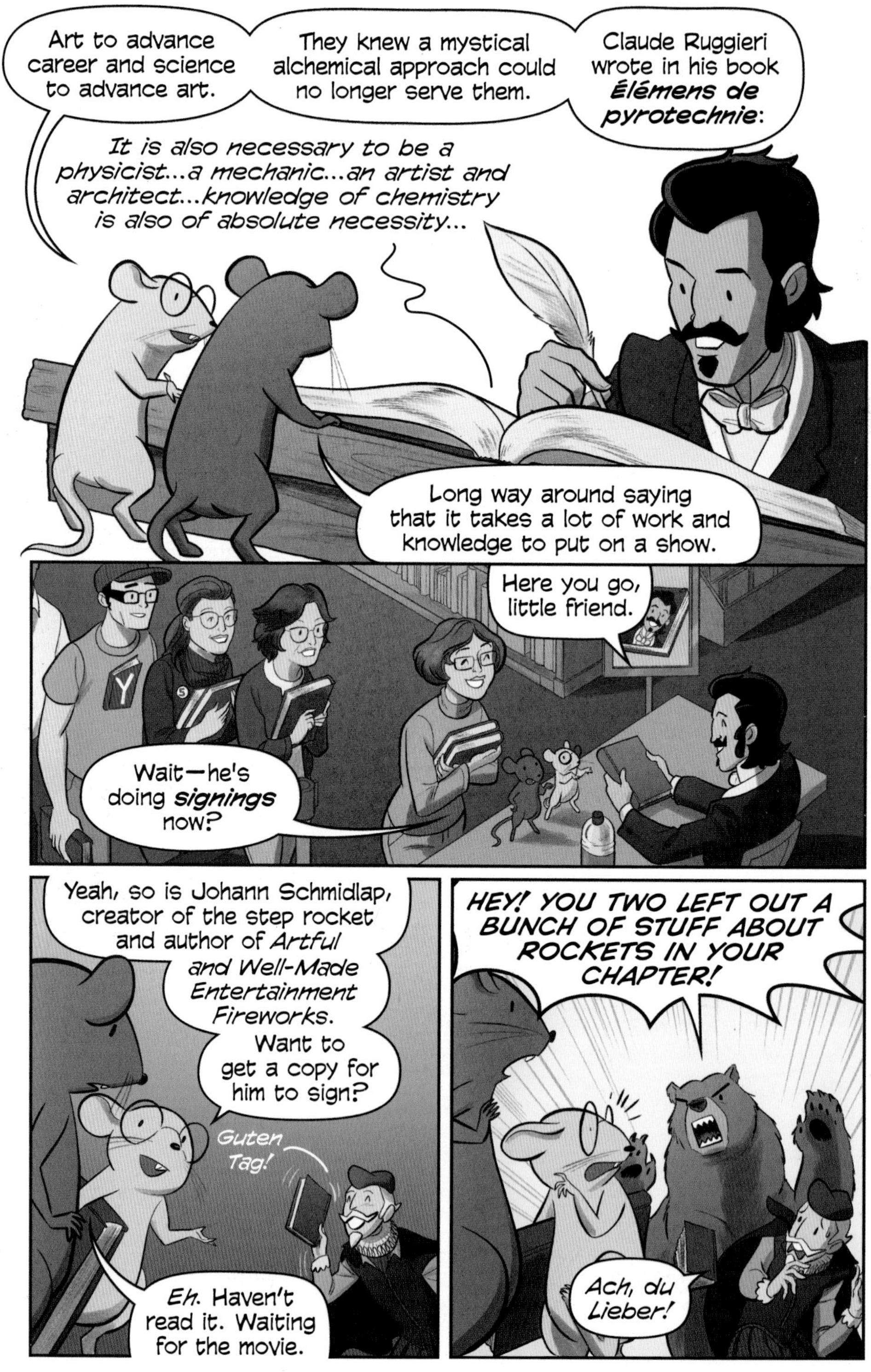

Art to advance career and science to advance art.
They knew a mystical alchemical approach could no longer serve them.
Claude Ruggieri wrote in his book ***Élémens de pyrotechnie***:
It is also necessary to be a physicist...a mechanic...an artist and architect...knowledge of chemistry is also of absolute necessity...
Long way around saying that it takes a lot of work and knowledge to put on a show.
Here you go, little friend.
Wait—he's doing ***signings*** now?
Yeah, so is Johann Schmidlap, creator of the step rocket and author of *Artful and Well-Made Entertainment Fireworks*.
Want to get a copy for him to sign?
Guten Tag!
Eh. Haven't read it. Waiting for the movie.
HEY! YOU TWO LEFT OUT A BUNCH OF STUFF ABOUT ROCKETS IN YOUR CHAPTER!
Ach, du Lieber!

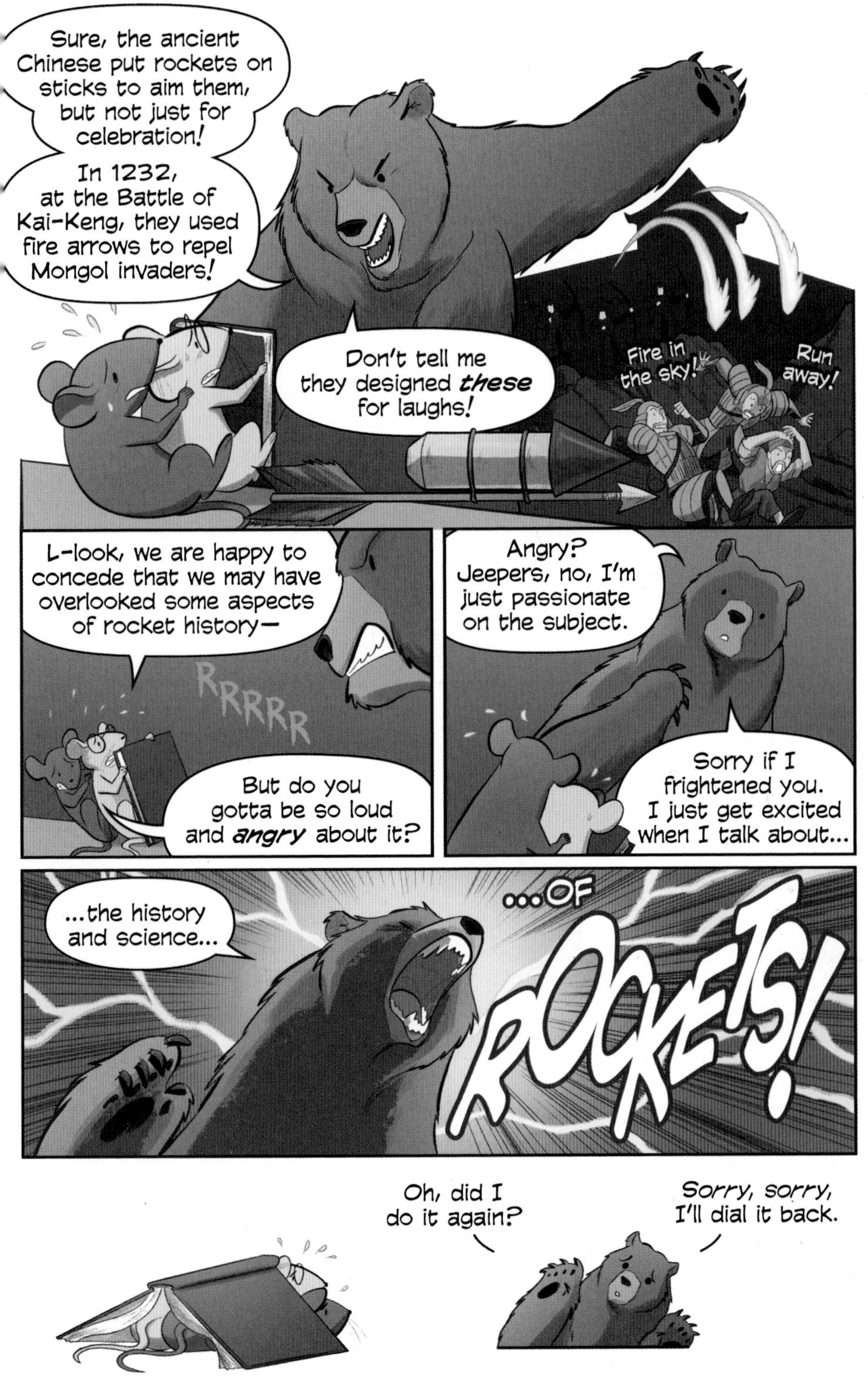
Sure, the ancient Chinese put rockets on sticks to aim them, but not just for celebration!
In 1232, at the Battle of Kai-Keng, they used fire arrows to repel Mongol invaders!
Don't tell me they designed *these* for laughs!
Fire in the sky!
Run away!
L-look, we are happy to concede that we may have overlooked some aspects of rocket history—
RRRRR
But do you gotta be so loud and *angry* about it?
Angry? Jeepers, no, I'm just passionate on the subject.
Sorry if I frightened you. I just get excited when I talk about...
...the history and science...
...OF ROCKETS!
Oh, did I do it again?
Sorry, sorry, I'll dial it back.

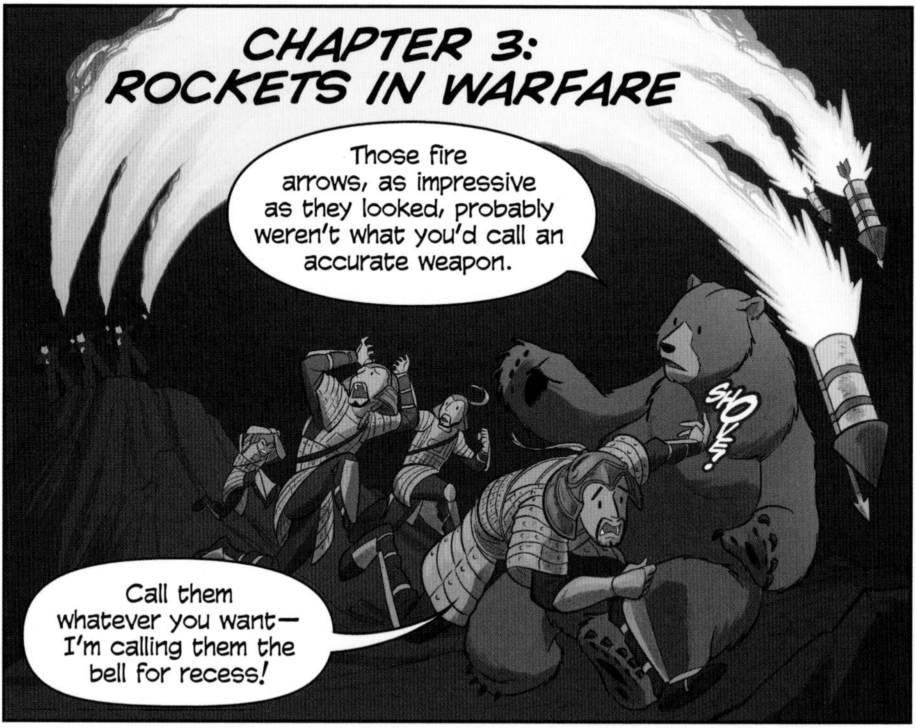
CHAPTER 3: ROCKETS IN WARFARE
Those fire arrows, as impressive as they looked, probably weren't what you'd call an accurate weapon.
SHOOP!
Call them whatever you want— I'm calling them the bell for recess!

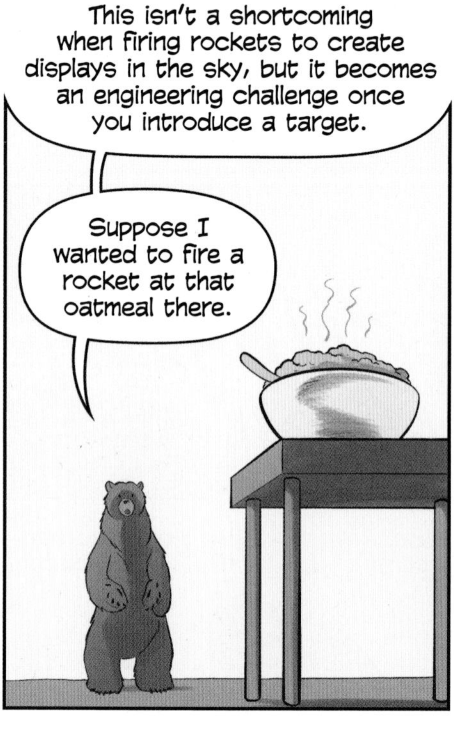
This isn't a shortcoming when firing rockets to create displays in the sky, but it becomes an engineering challenge once you introduce a target.
Suppose I wanted to fire a rocket at that oatmeal there.

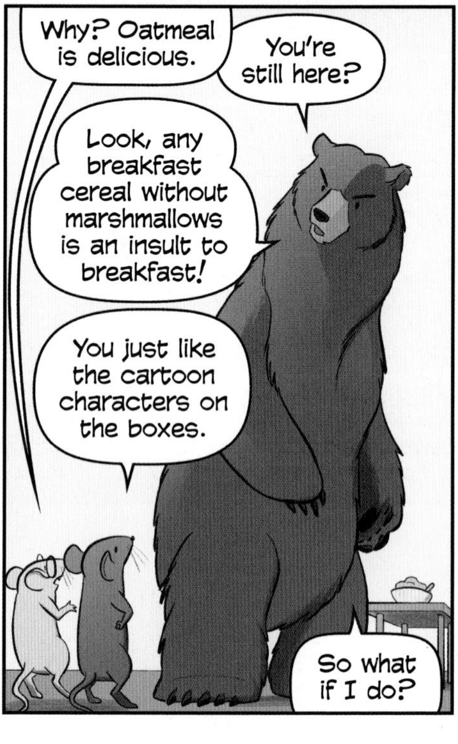
Why? Oatmeal is delicious.
You're still here?
Look, any breakfast cereal without marshmallows is an insult to breakfast!
You just like the cartoon characters on the boxes.
So what if I do?

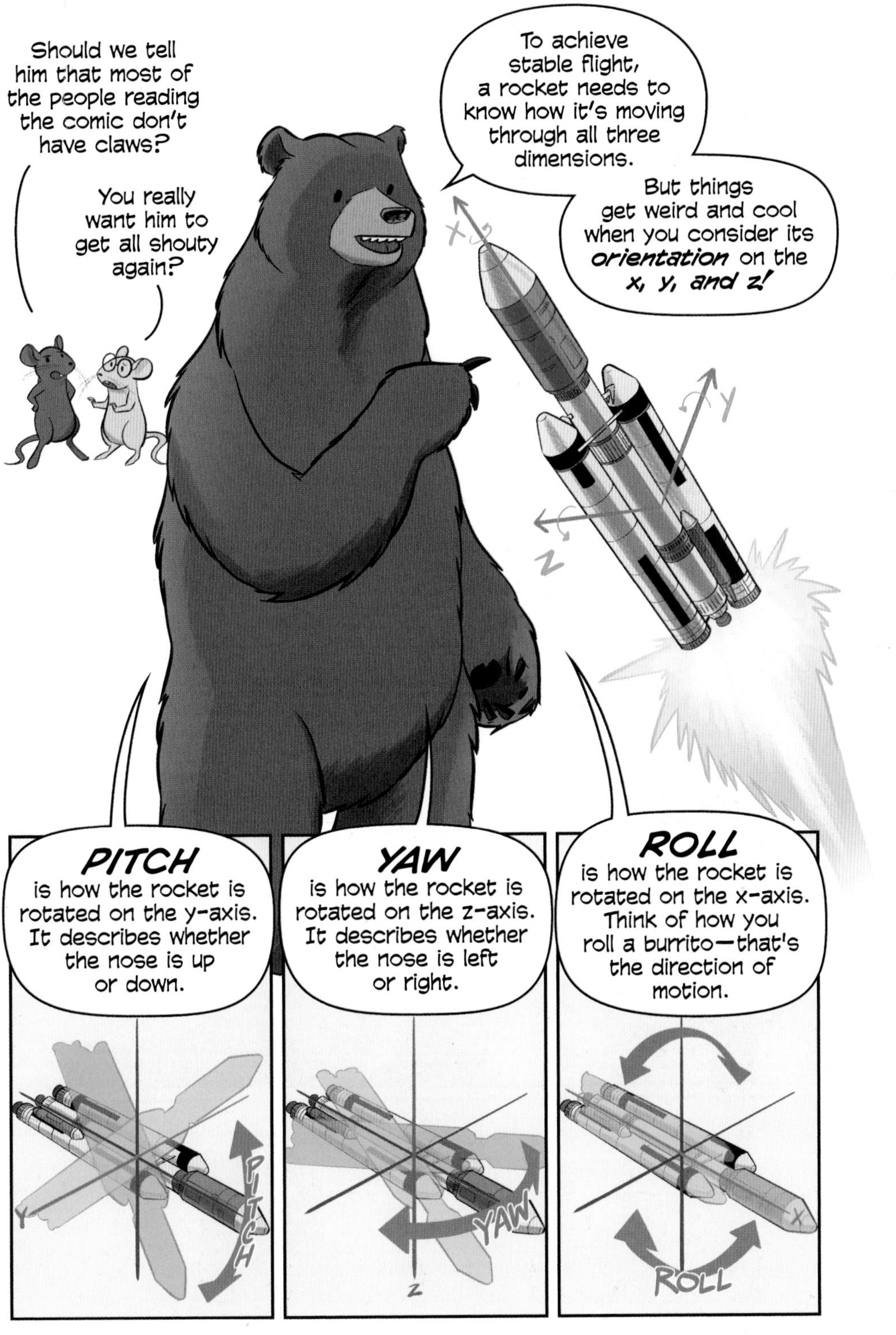

Should we tell him that most of the people reading the comic don't have claws?
You really want him to get all shouty again?
To achieve stable flight, a rocket needs to know how it's moving through all three dimensions.
But things get weird and cool when you consider its *orientation* on the *x, y, and z!*
X
Y
Z
PITCH is how the rocket is rotated on the y-axis. It describes whether the nose is up or down.
Y
PITCH
YAW is how the rocket is rotated on the z-axis. It describes whether the nose is left or right.
YAW
Z
ROLL is how the rocket is rotated on the x-axis. Think of how you roll a burrito—that's the direction of motion.
X
ROLL

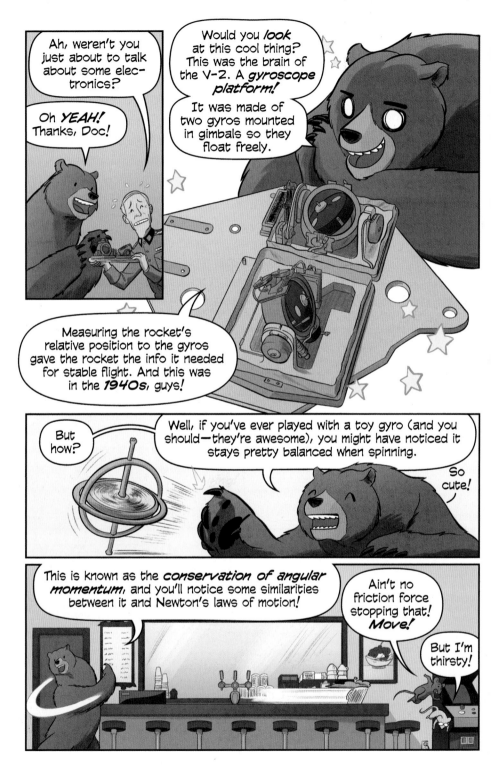

Ah, weren't you just about to talk about some electronics?

Oh *YEAH!* Thanks, Doc!

Would you *look* at this cool thing? This was the brain of the V-2. A *gyroscope platform!*

It was made of two gyros mounted in gimbals so they float freely.

Measuring the rocket's relative position to the gyros gave the rocket the info it needed for stable flight. And this was in the *1940s*, guys!

But how?

Well, if you've ever played with a toy gyro (and you should—they're awesome), you might have noticed it stays pretty balanced when spinning.

So cute!

This is known as the *conservation of angular momentum,* and you'll notice some similarities between it and Newton's laws of motion!

Ain't no friction force stopping that! *Move!*

But I'm thirsty!

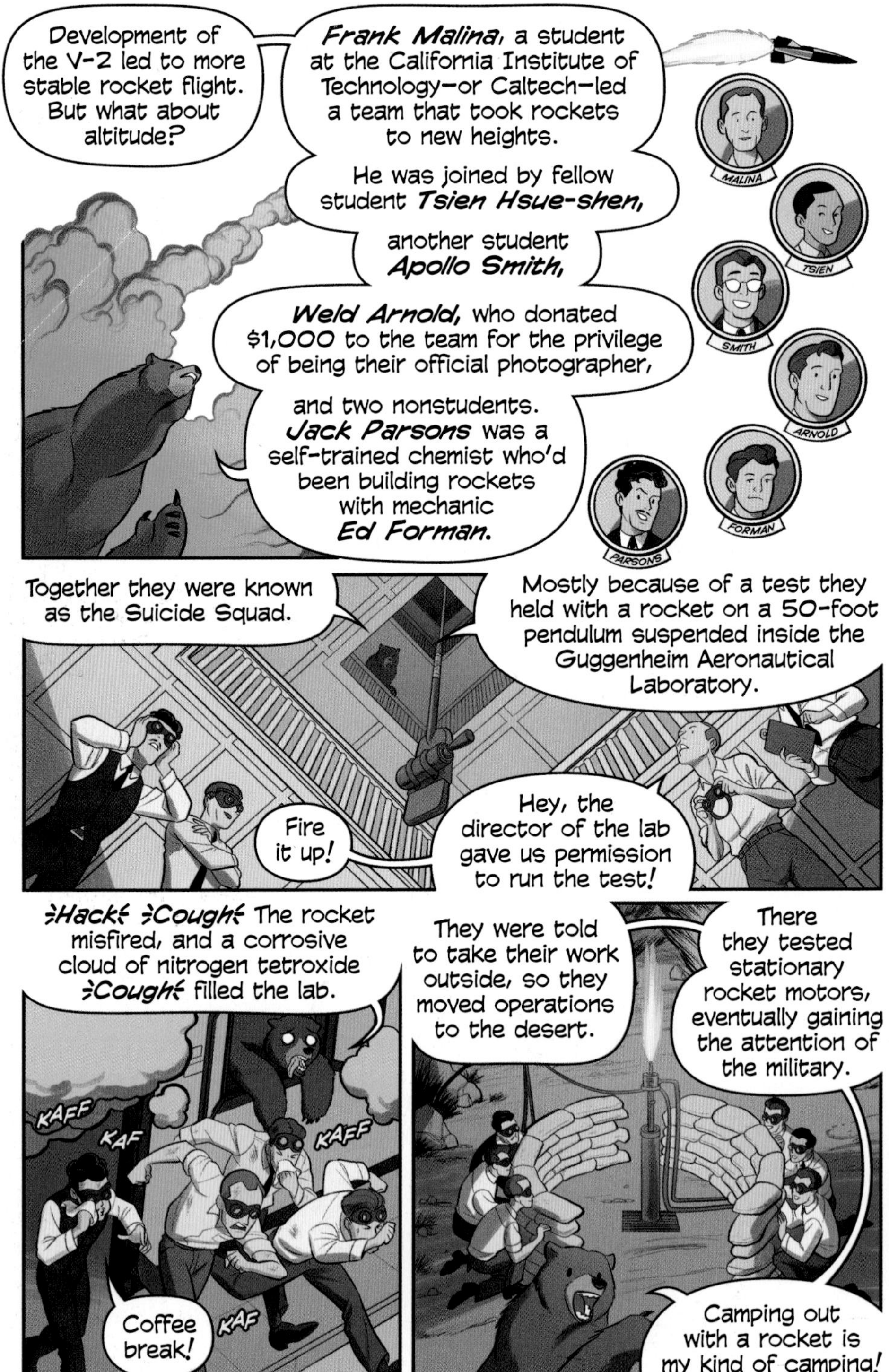
Development of the V-2 led to more stable rocket flight. But what about altitude?
Frank Malina, a student at the California Institute of Technology—or Caltech—led a team that took rockets to new heights.
He was joined by fellow student Tsien Hsue-shen,
another student Apollo Smith,
Weld Arnold, who donated $1,000 to the team for the privilege of being their official photographer,
and two nonstudents. Jack Parsons was a self-trained chemist who'd been building rockets with mechanic Ed Forman.
MALINA
TSIEN
SMITH
ARNOLD
FORMAN
PARSONS
Together they were known as the Suicide Squad.
Mostly because of a test they held with a rocket on a 50-foot pendulum suspended inside the Guggenheim Aeronautical Laboratory.
Fire it up!
Hey, the director of the lab gave us permission to run the test!
Hack *Cough* The rocket misfired, and a corrosive cloud of nitrogen tetroxide *Cough* filled the lab.
KAFF
KAF
KAFF
Coffee break!
KAF
They were told to take their work outside, so they moved operations to the desert.
There they tested stationary rocket motors, eventually gaining the attention of the military.
Camping out with a rocket is my kind of camping!

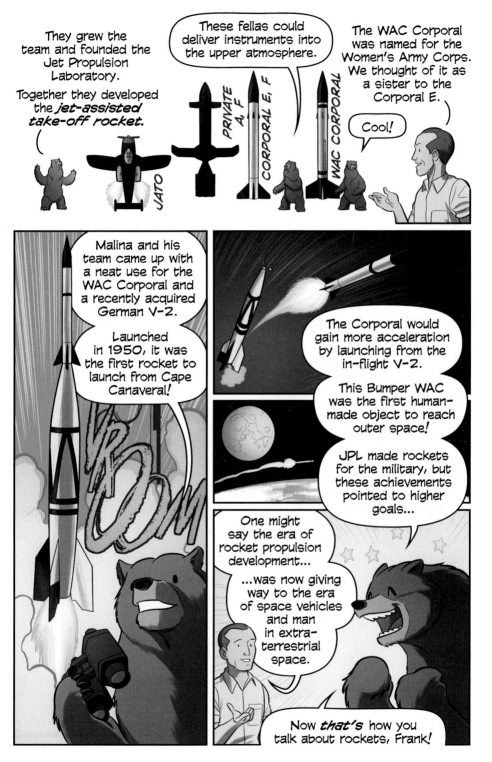

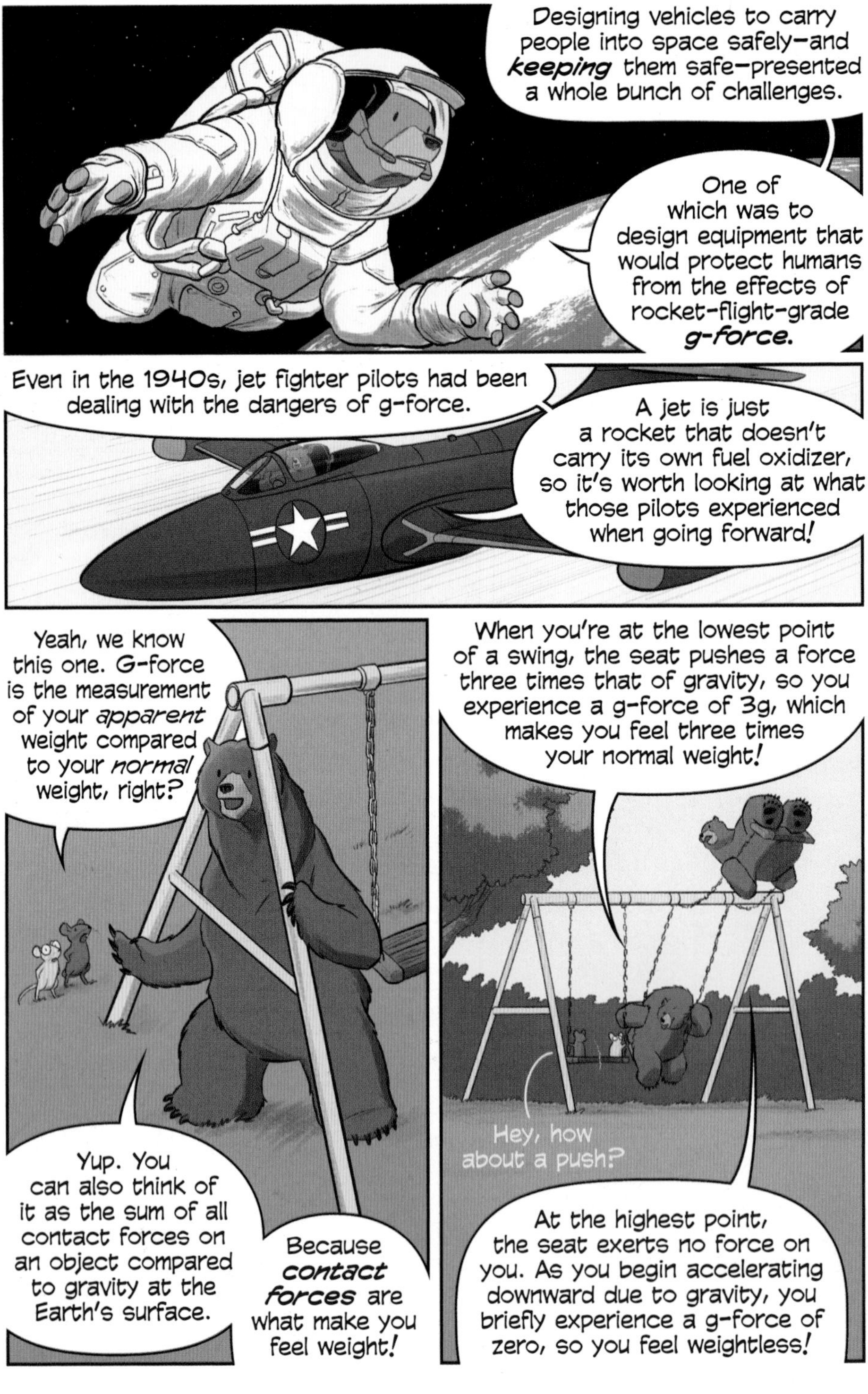
Designing vehicles to carry people into space safely—and *keeping* them safe—presented a whole bunch of challenges.
One of which was to design equipment that would protect humans from the effects of rocket-flight-grade ***g-force.***
Even in the 1940s, jet fighter pilots had been dealing with the dangers of g-force.
A jet is just a rocket that doesn't carry its own fuel oxidizer, so it's worth looking at what those pilots experienced when going forward!
Yeah, we know this one. G-force is the measurement of your *apparent* weight compared to your *normal* weight, right?
Yup. You can also think of it as the sum of all contact forces on an object compared to gravity at the Earth's surface.
Because ***contact forces*** are what make you feel weight!
When you're at the lowest point of a swing, the seat pushes a force three times that of gravity, so you experience a g-force of 3g, which makes you feel three times your normal weight!
Hey, how about a push?
At the highest point, the seat exerts no force on you. As you begin accelerating downward due to gravity, you briefly experience a g-force of zero, so you feel weightless!

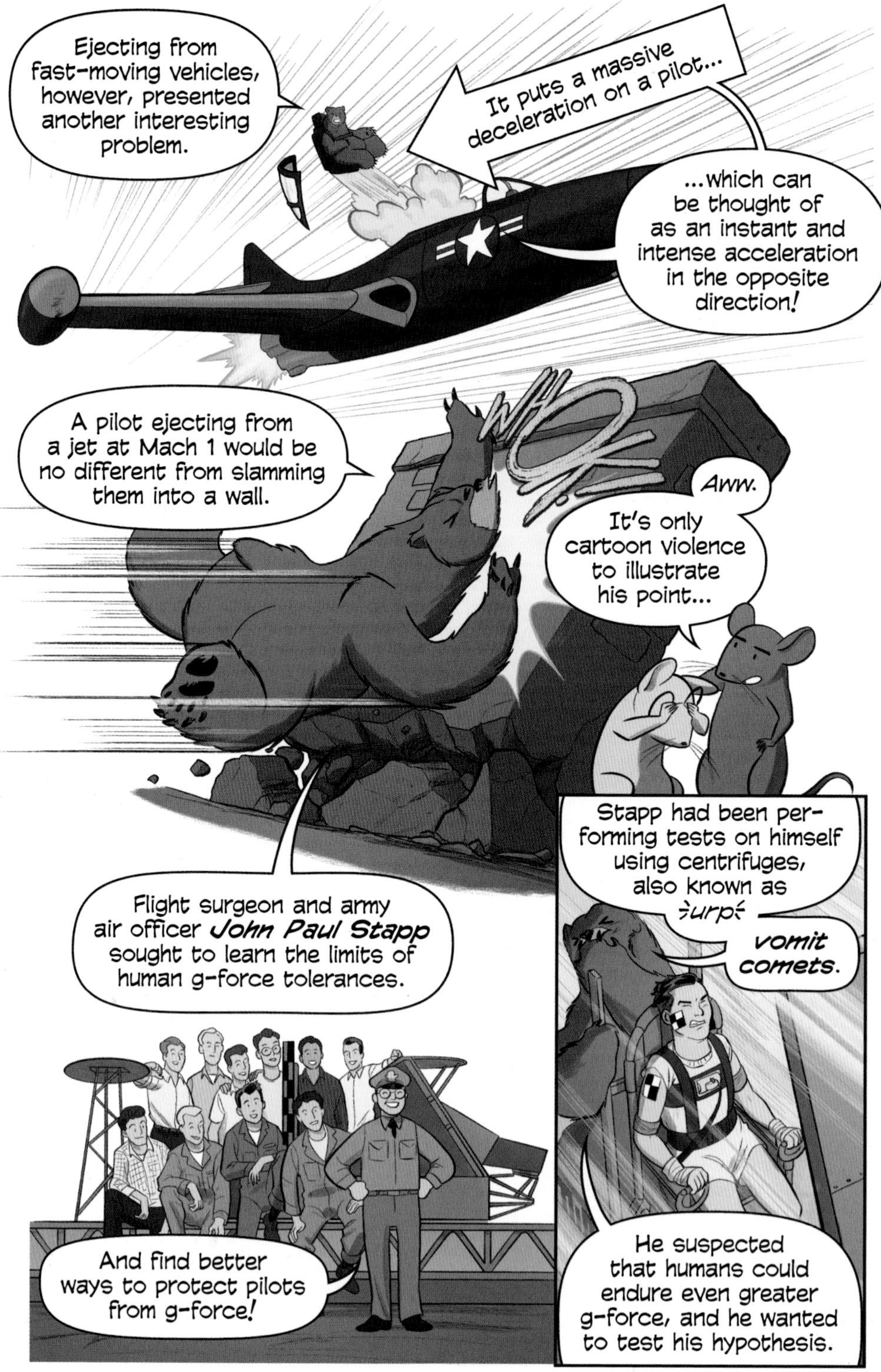
Ejecting from fast-moving vehicles, however, presented another interesting problem.
It puts a massive deceleration on a pilot...
...which can be thought of as an instant and intense acceleration in the opposite direction!
A pilot ejecting from a jet at Mach 1 would be no different from slamming them into a wall.
WHOK
Aww.
It's only cartoon violence to illustrate his point...
Flight surgeon and army air officer John Paul Stapp sought to learn the limits of human g-force tolerances.
Stapp had been performing tests on himself using centrifuges, also known as
urp
vomit comets.
And find better ways to protect pilots from g-force!
He suspected that humans could endure even greater g-force, and he wanted to test his hypothesis.

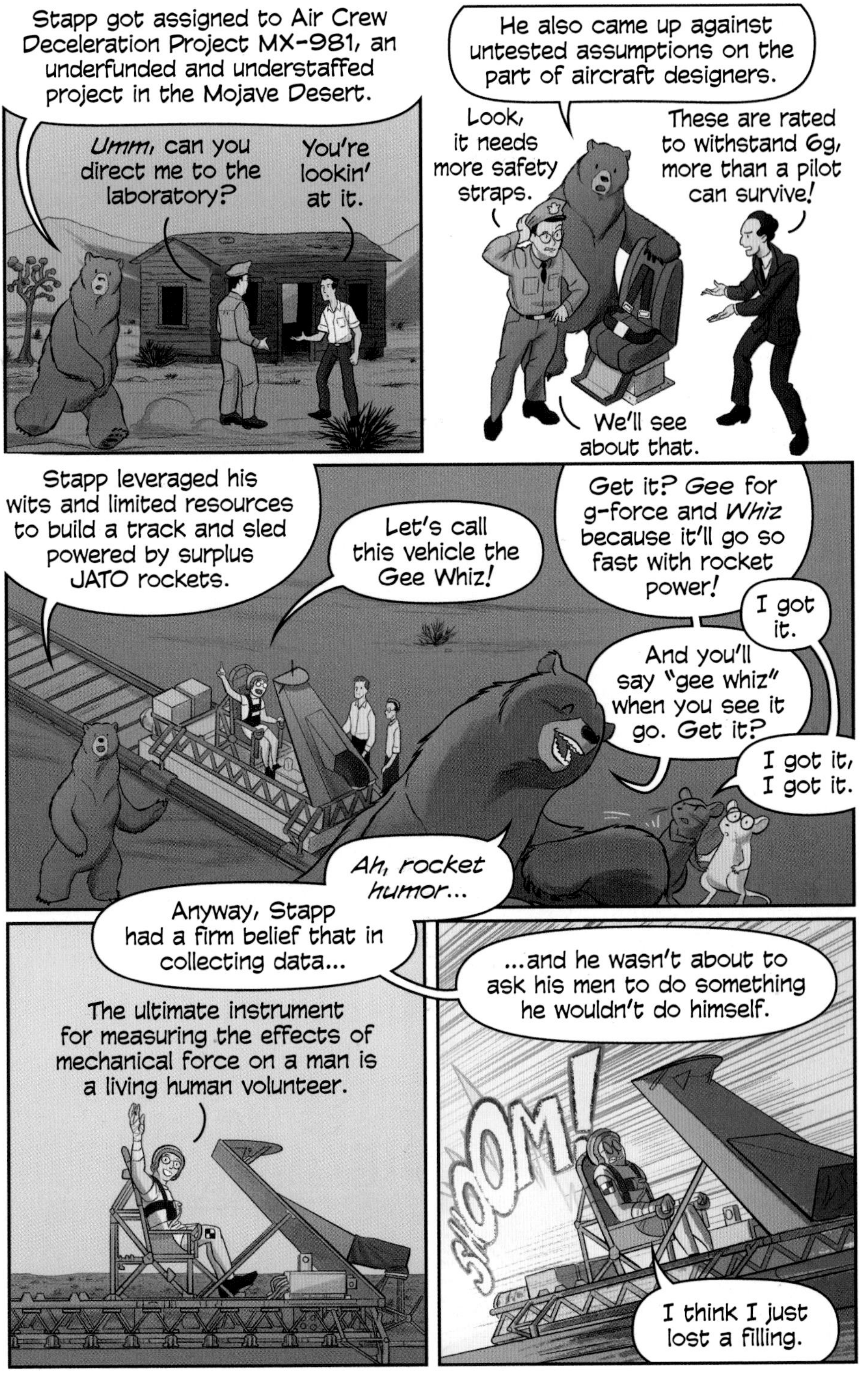
Stapp got assigned to Air Crew Deceleration Project MX-981, an underfunded and understaffed project in the Mojave Desert.
Umm, can you direct me to the laboratory?
You're lookin' at it.
He also came up against untested assumptions on the part of aircraft designers.
Look, it needs more safety straps.
These are rated to withstand 6g, more than a pilot can survive!
We'll see about that.
Stapp leveraged his wits and limited resources to build a track and sled powered by surplus JATO rockets.
Let's call this vehicle the Gee Whiz!
Get it? Gee for g-force and Whiz because it'll go so fast with rocket power!
I got it.
And you'll say "gee whiz" when you see it go. Get it?
I got it, I got it.
Ah, rocket humor...
Anyway, Stapp had a firm belief that in collecting data...
The ultimate instrument for measuring the effects of mechanical force on a man is a living human volunteer.
...and he wasn't about to ask his men to do something he wouldn't do himself.
SHOOOM!
I think I just lost a filling.

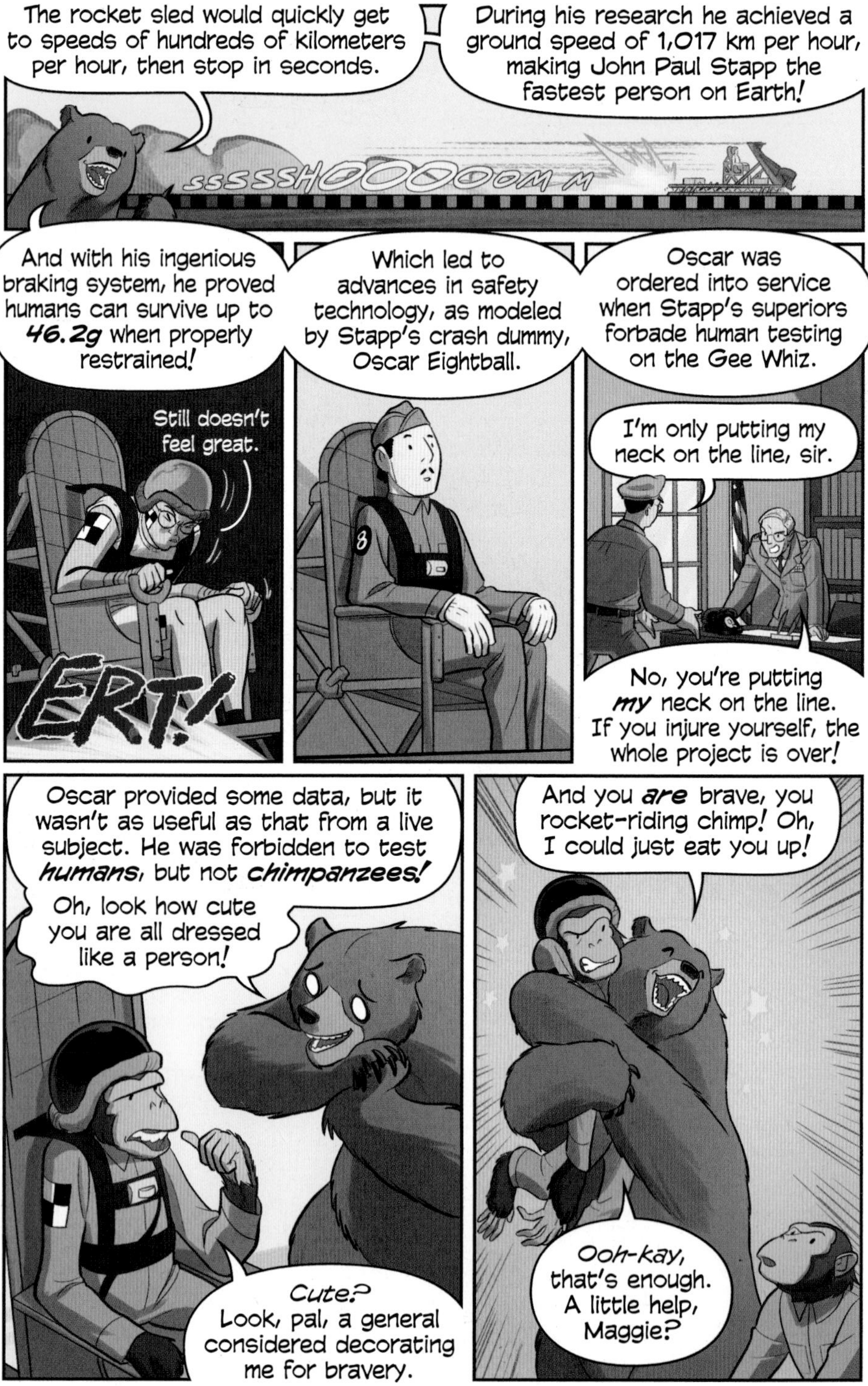
The rocket sled would quickly get to speeds of hundreds of kilometers per hour, then stop in seconds.
During his research he achieved a ground speed of 1,017 km per hour, making John Paul Stapp the fastest person on Earth!
ssSSSSHOOOOOOOM M
And with his ingenious braking system, he proved humans can survive up to 46.2g when properly restrained!
Still doesn't feel great.
ERT!
Which led to advances in safety technology, as modeled by Stapp's crash dummy, Oscar Eightball.
Oscar was ordered into service when Stapp's superiors forbade human testing on the Gee Whiz.
I'm only putting my neck on the line, sir.
No, you're putting my neck on the line. If you injure yourself, the whole project is over!
Oscar provided some data, but it wasn't as useful as that from a live subject. He was forbidden to test humans, but not chimpanzees!
Oh, look how cute you are all dressed like a person!
Cute? Look, pal, a general considered decorating me for bravery.
And you are brave, you rocket-riding chimp! Oh, I could just eat you up!
Ooh-kay, that's enough. A little help, Maggie?

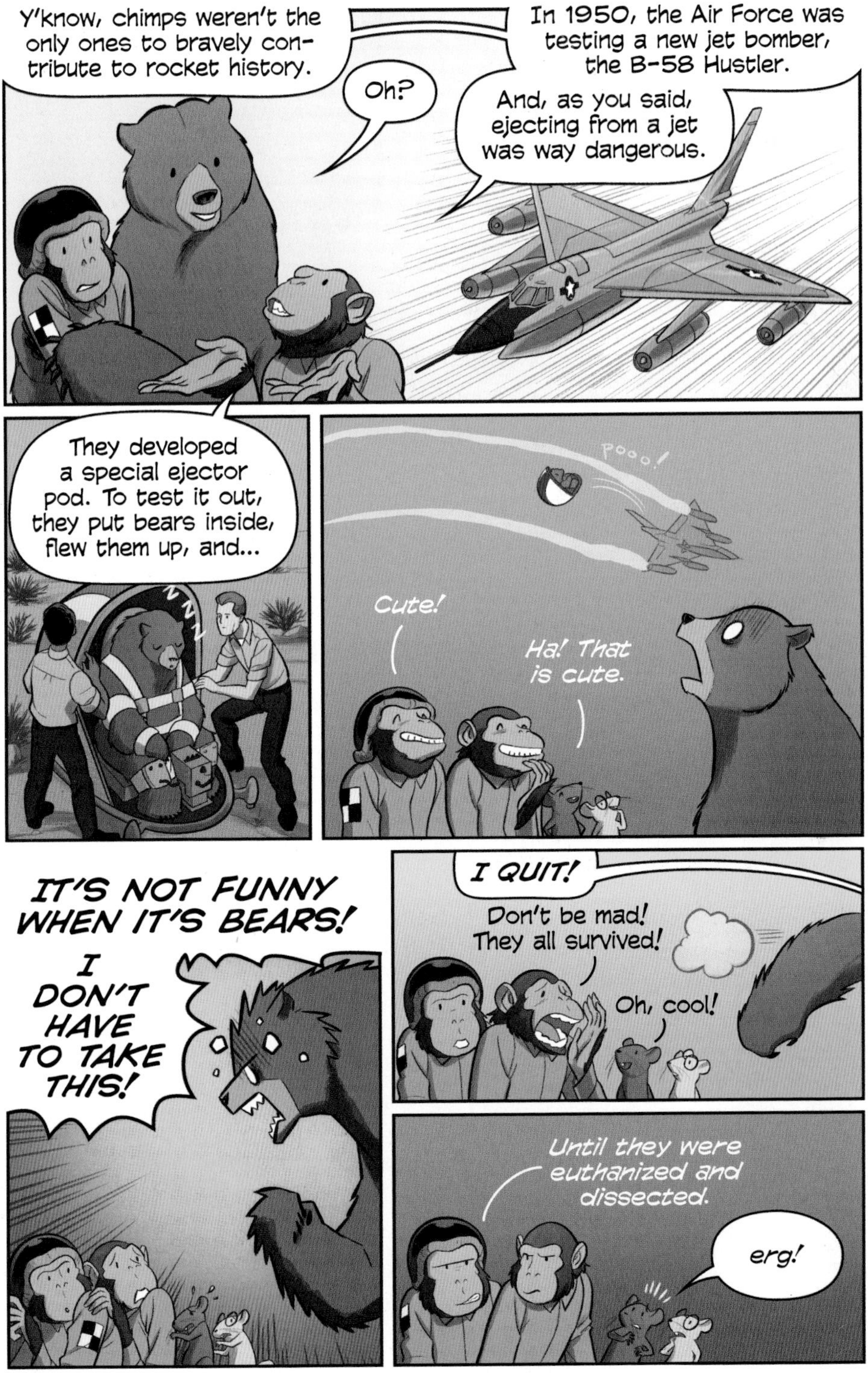
Y'know, chimps weren't the only ones to bravely contribute to rocket history.
Oh?
In 1950, the Air Force was testing a new jet bomber, the B-58 Hustler.
And, as you said, ejecting from a jet was way dangerous.
They developed a special ejector pod. To test it out, they put bears inside, flew them up, and...
POOO!
Cute!
Ha! That is cute.
IT'S NOT FUNNY WHEN IT'S BEARS!
I DON'T HAVE TO TAKE THIS!
I QUIT!
Don't be mad! They all survived!
Oh, cool!
Until they were euthanized and dissected.
erg!

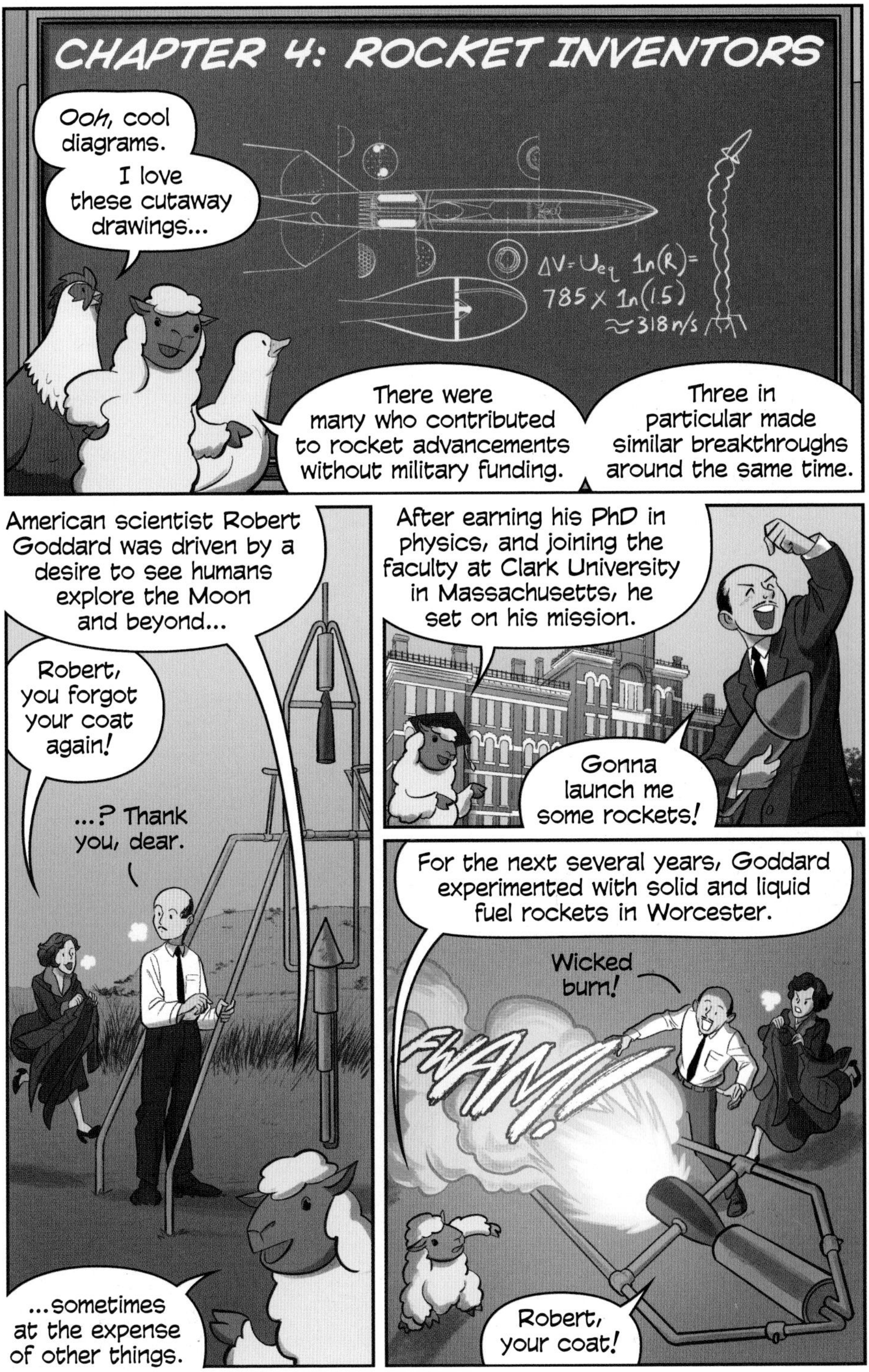
CHAPTER 4: ROCKET INVENTORS
Ooh, cool diagrams.
I love these cutaway drawings...
ΔV=Ueq ln(R)= 785 x ln(1.5) ≈318 m/s
There were many who contributed to rocket advancements without military funding.
Three in particular made similar breakthroughs around the same time.
American scientist Robert Goddard was driven by a desire to see humans explore the Moon and beyond...
Robert, you forgot your coat again!
...? Thank you, dear.
...sometimes at the expense of other things.
After earning his PhD in physics, and joining the faculty at Clark University in Massachusetts, he set on his mission.
Gonna launch me some rockets!
For the next several years, Goddard experimented with solid and liquid fuel rockets in Worcester.
Wicked burn!
FWAM!!
Robert, your coat!

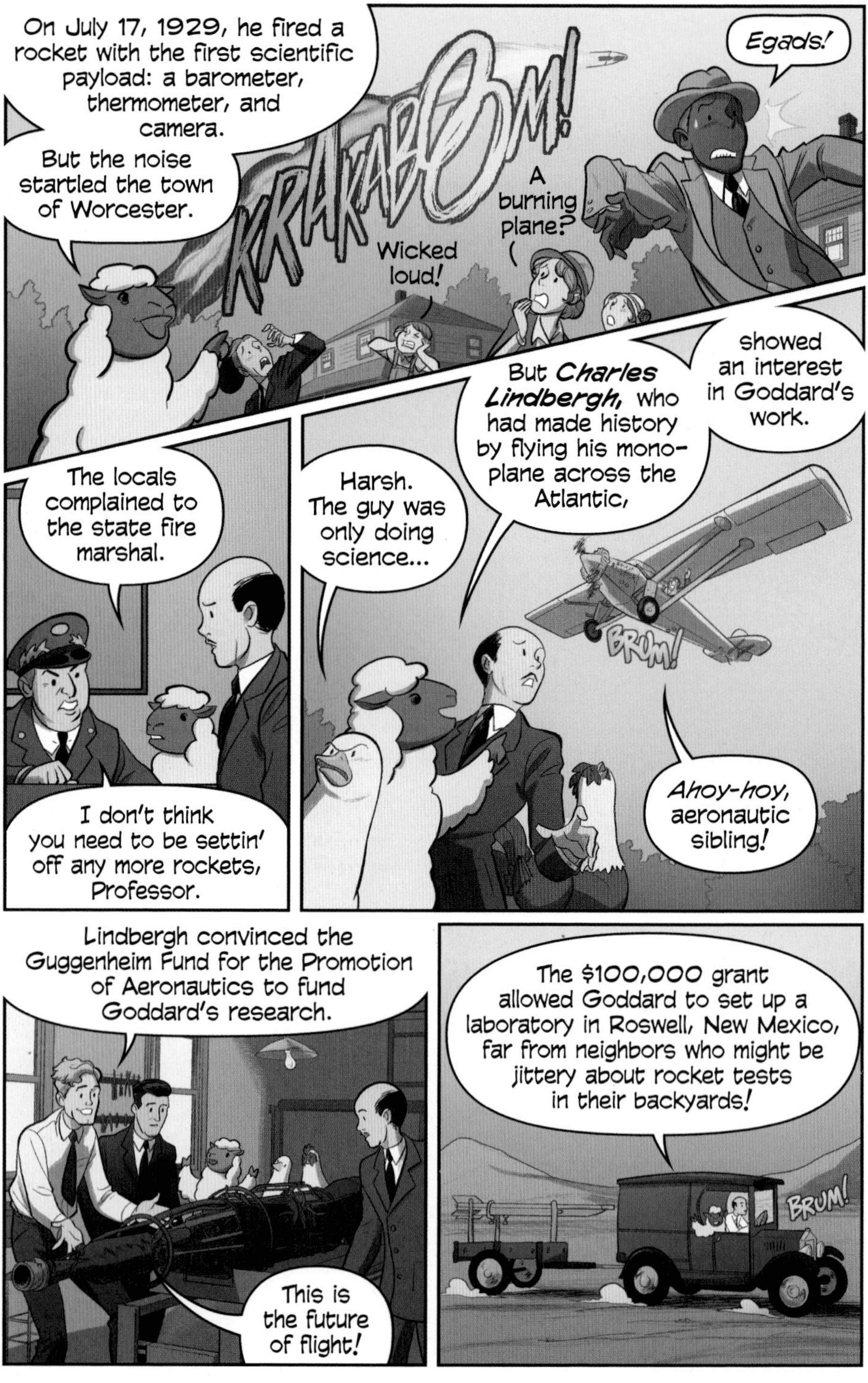

On July 17, 1929, he fired a rocket with the first scientific payload: a barometer, thermometer, and camera.
But the noise startled the town of Worcester.
KRAKABOOM!
Wicked loud!
A burning plane?
Egads!
The locals complained to the state fire marshal.
I don't think you need to be settin' off any more rockets, Professor.
Harsh. The guy was only doing science...
But *Charles Lindbergh,* who had made history by flying his mono-plane across the Atlantic,
showed an interest in Goddard's work.
BRUM!
Ahoy-hoy, aeronautic sibling!
Lindbergh convinced the Guggenheim Fund for the Promotion of Aeronautics to fund Goddard's research.
This is the future of flight!
The $100,000 grant allowed Goddard to set up a laboratory in Roswell, New Mexico, far from neighbors who might be jittery about rocket tests in their backyards!
BRUM!

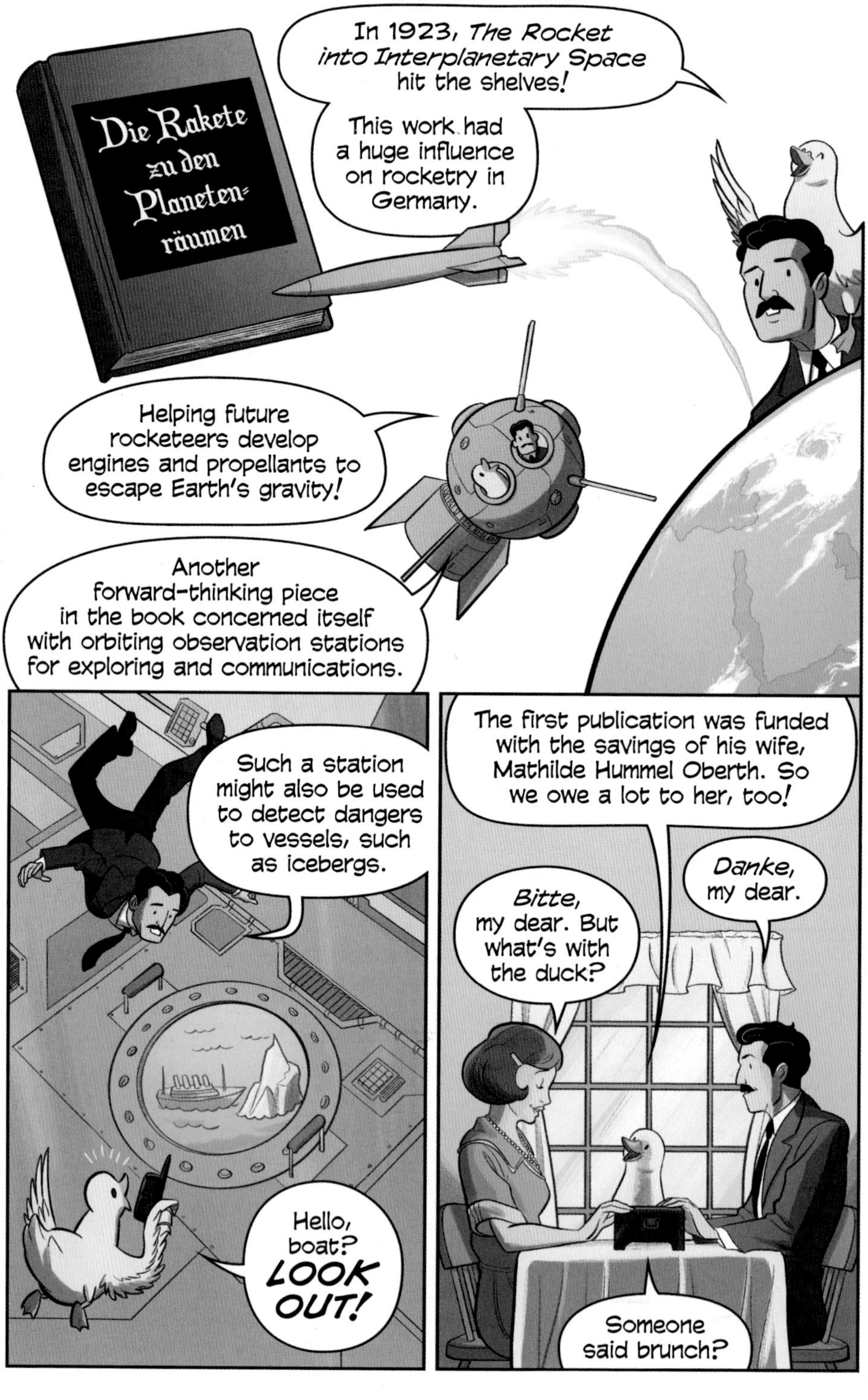

Die Rakete zu den Planeten-räumen
In 1923, *The Rocket into Interplanetary Space* hit the shelves!
This work had a huge influence on rocketry in Germany.
Helping future rocketeers develop engines and propellants to escape Earth's gravity!
Another forward-thinking piece in the book concerned itself with orbiting observation stations for exploring and communications.
Such a station might also be used to detect dangers to vessels, such as icebergs.
Hello, boat? *LOOK OUT!*
The first publication was funded with the savings of his wife, Mathilde Hummel Oberth. So we owe a lot to her, too!
Danke, my dear.
Bitte, my dear. But what's with the duck?
Someone said brunch?

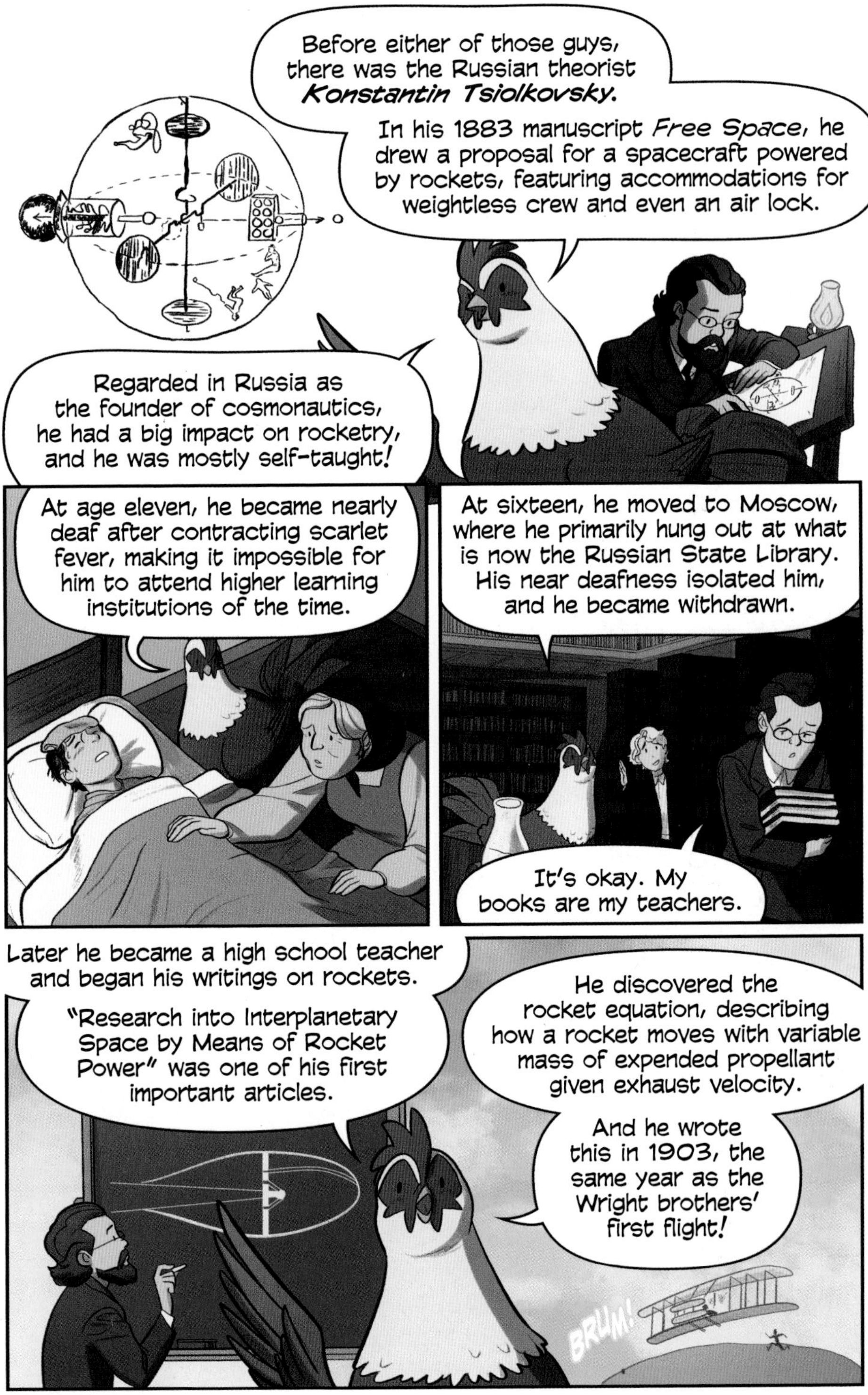
Before either of those guys, there was the Russian theorist ***Konstantin Tsiolkovsky.***
In his 1883 manuscript *Free Space,* he drew a proposal for a spacecraft powered by rockets, featuring accommodations for weightless crew and even an air lock.
Regarded in Russia as the founder of cosmonautics, he had a big impact on rocketry, and he was mostly self-taught!
At age eleven, he became nearly deaf after contracting scarlet fever, making it impossible for him to attend higher learning institutions of the time.
At sixteen, he moved to Moscow, where he primarily hung out at what is now the Russian State Library. His near deafness isolated him, and he became withdrawn.
It's okay. My books are my teachers.
Later he became a high school teacher and began his writings on rockets.
"Research into Interplanetary Space by Means of Rocket Power" was one of his first important articles.
He discovered the rocket equation, describing how a rocket moves with variable mass of expended propellant given exhaust velocity.
And he wrote this in 1903, the same year as the Wright brothers' first flight!
BRUM!

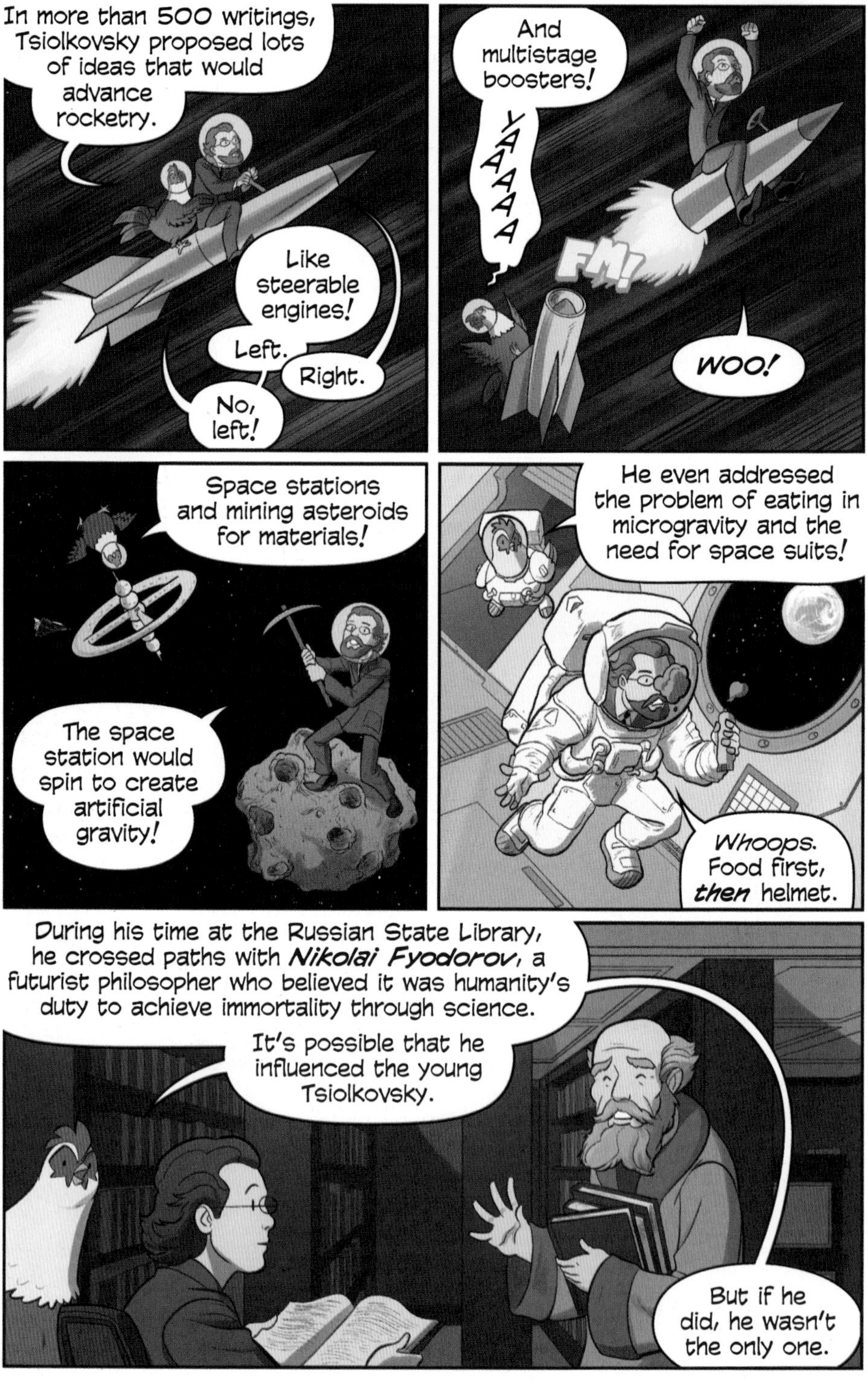

In more than 500 writings, Tsiolkovsky proposed lots of ideas that would advance rocketry.
Like steerable engines!
Left.
Right.
No, left!
And multistage boosters!
YAAAAAA
FM!
WOO!
Space stations and mining asteroids for materials!
The space station would spin to create artificial gravity!
He even addressed the problem of eating in microgravity and the need for space suits!
Whoops. Food first, then helmet.
During his time at the Russian State Library, he crossed paths with Nikolai Fyodorov, a futurist philosopher who believed it was humanity's duty to achieve immortality through science.
It's possible that he influenced the young Tsiolkovsky.
But if he did, he wasn't the only one.

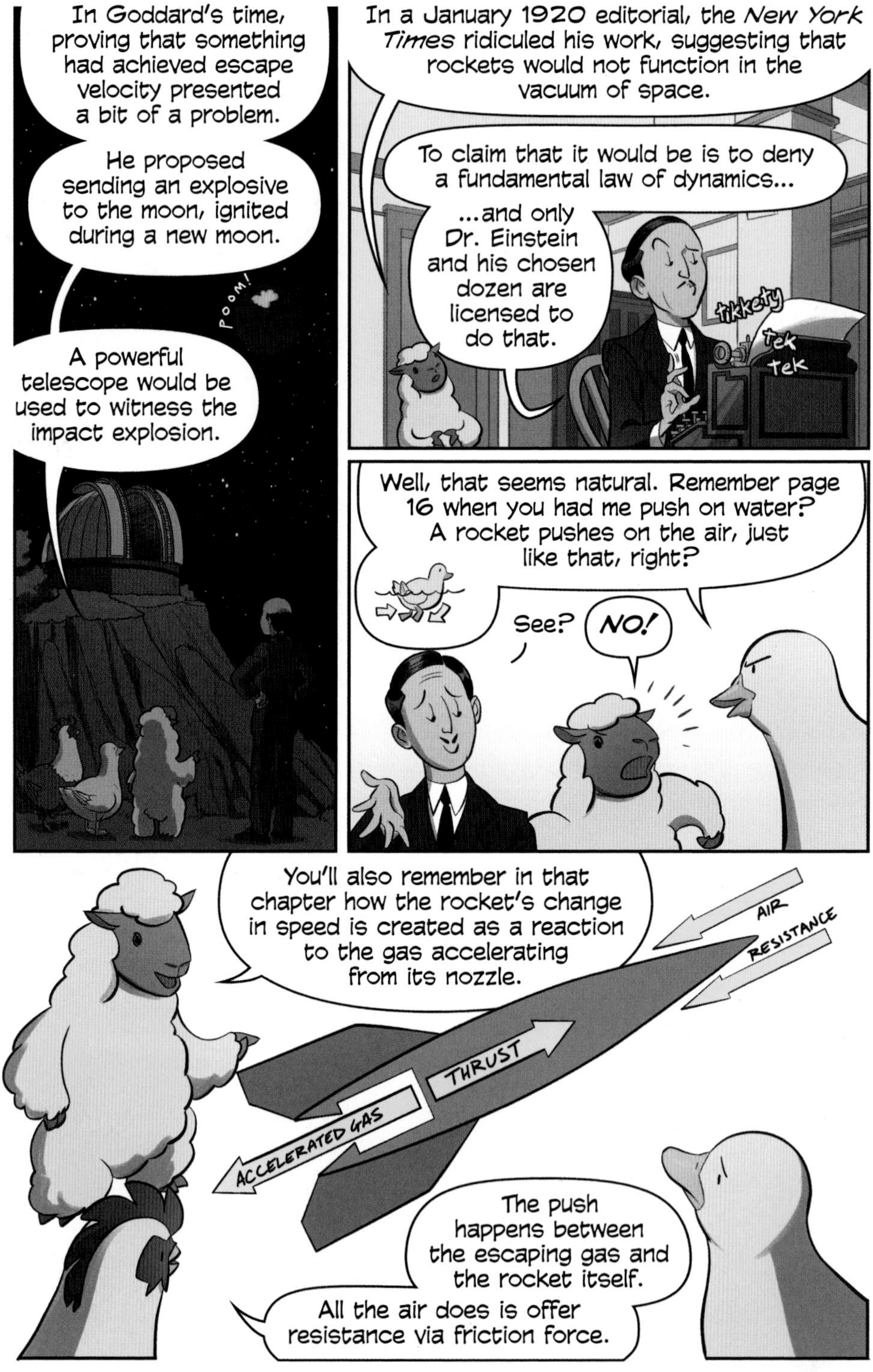
In Goddard's time, proving that something had achieved escape velocity presented a bit of a problem.
He proposed sending an explosive to the moon, ignited during a new moon.
POOM!
A powerful telescope would be used to witness the impact explosion.
In a January 1920 editorial, the *New York Times* ridiculed his work, suggesting that rockets would not function in the vacuum of space.
To claim that it would be is to deny a fundamental law of dynamics...
...and only Dr. Einstein and his chosen dozen are licensed to do that.
tikkety
tek
tek
Well, that seems natural. Remember page 16 when you had me push on water? A rocket pushes on the air, just like that, right?
See?
NO!
You'll also remember in that chapter how the rocket's change in speed is created as a reaction to the gas accelerating from its nozzle.
AIR
RESISTANCE
THRUST
ACCELERATED GAS
The push happens between the escaping gas and the rocket itself.
All the air does is offer resistance via friction force.

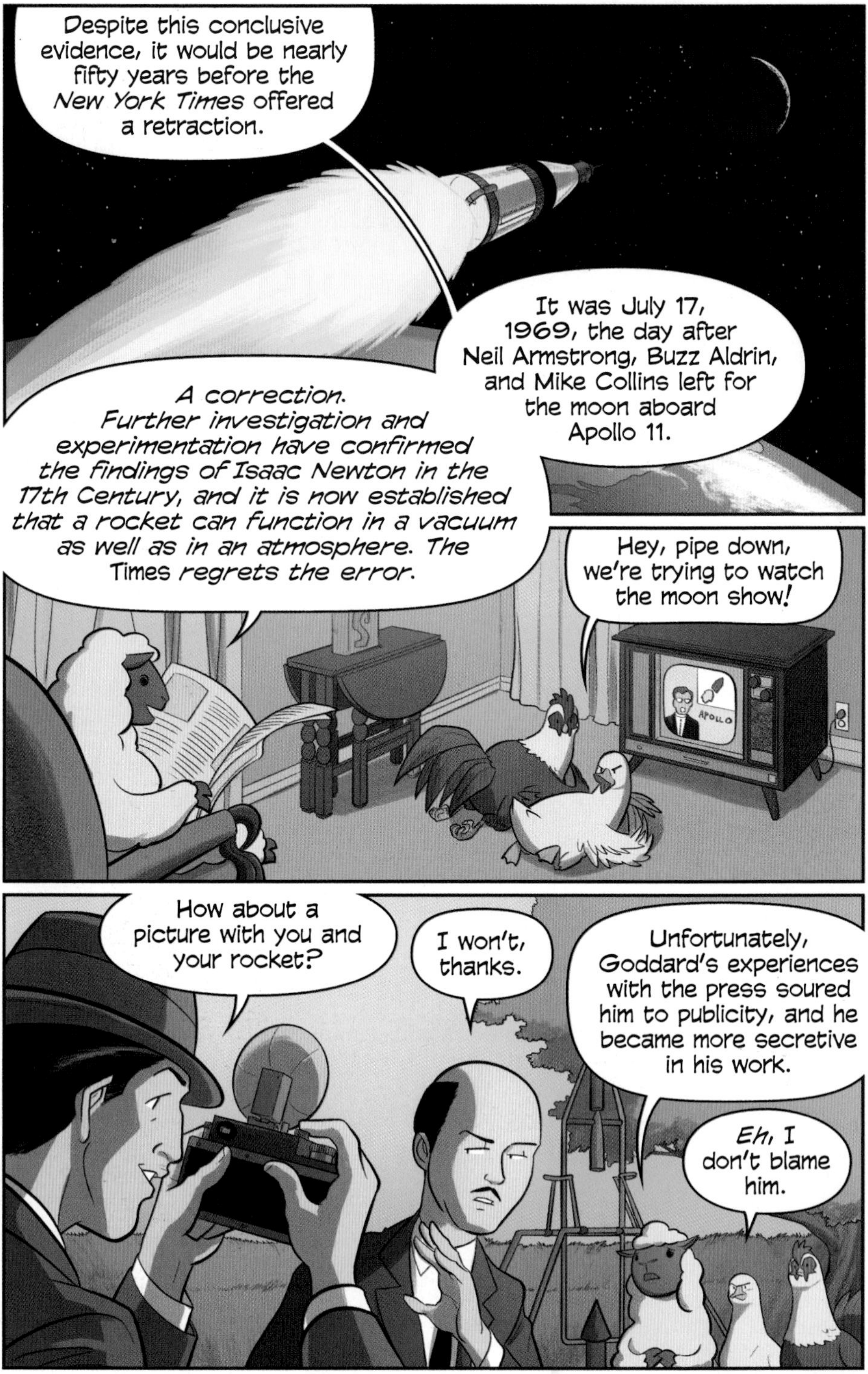
Despite this conclusive evidence, it would be nearly fifty years before the *New York Times* offered a retraction.
It was July 17, 1969, the day after Neil Armstrong, Buzz Aldrin, and Mike Collins left for the moon aboard Apollo 11.
A correction. Further investigation and experimentation have confirmed the findings of Isaac Newton in the 17th Century, and it is now established that a rocket can function in a vacuum as well as in an atmosphere. The Times *regrets the error.*
Hey, pipe down, we're trying to watch the moon show!
APOLLO
How about a picture with you and your rocket?
I won't, thanks.
Unfortunately, Goddard's experiences with the press soured him to publicity, and he became more secretive in his work.
Eh, I don't blame him.

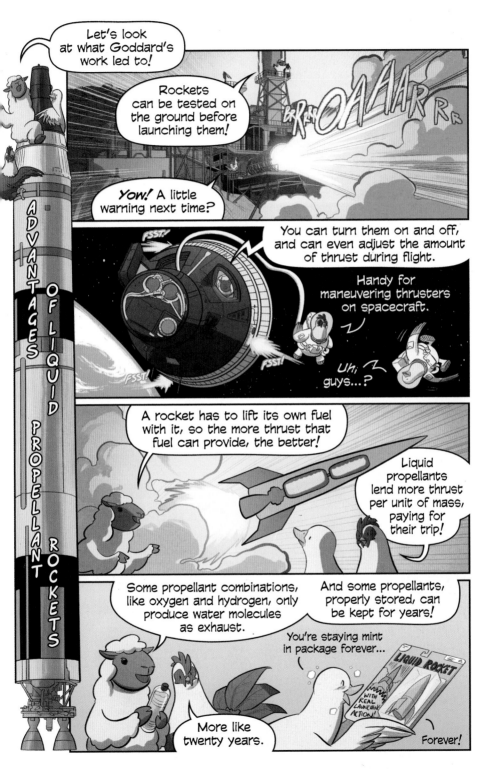

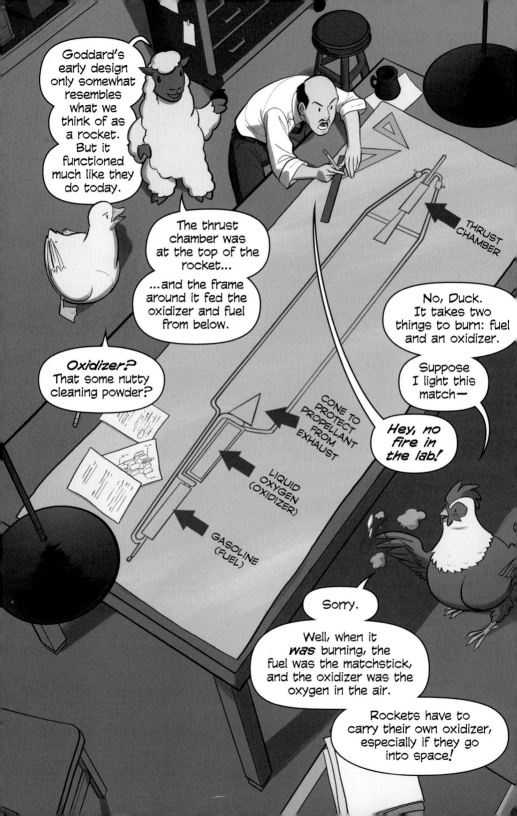

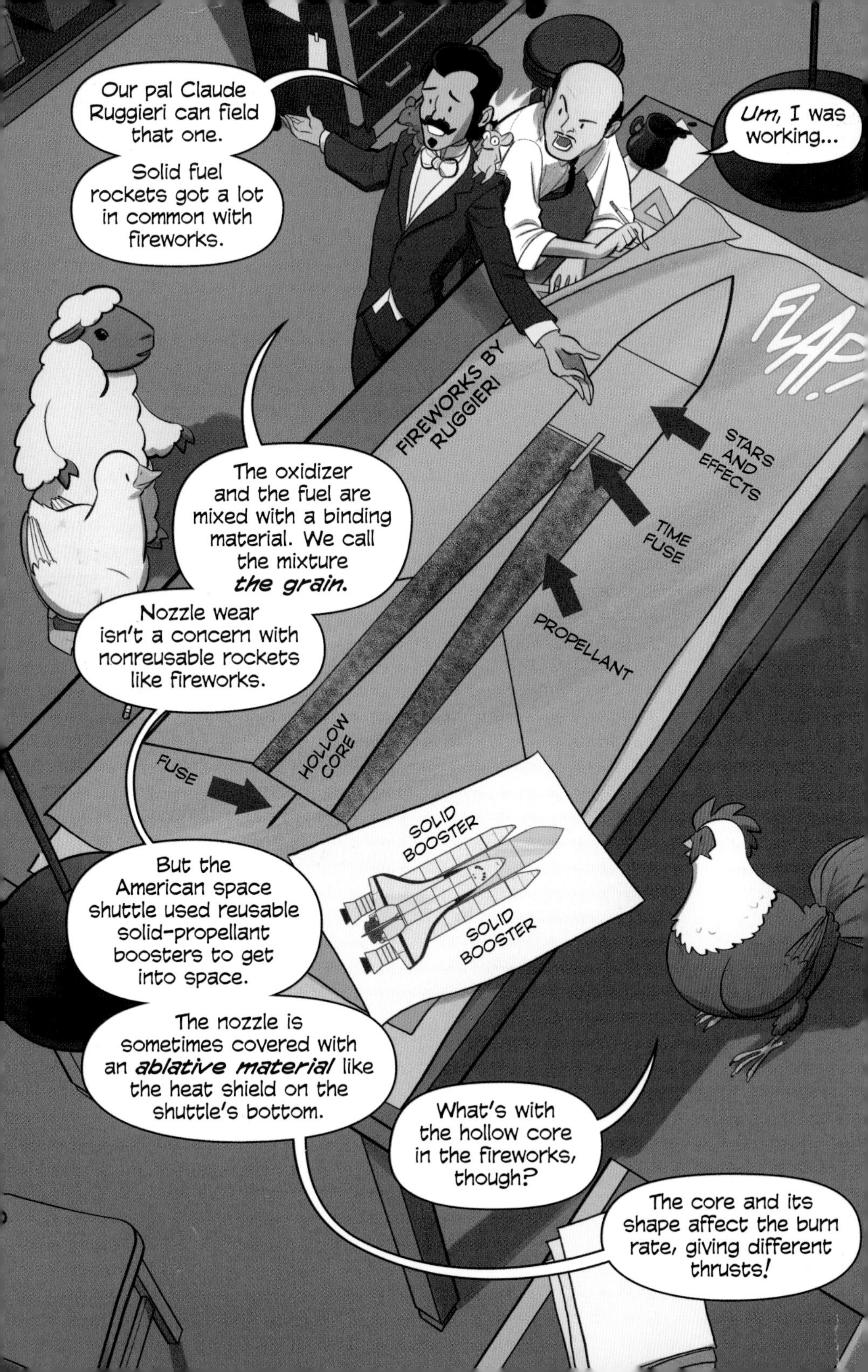
Our pal Claude Ruggieri can field that one.
Solid fuel rockets got a lot in common with fireworks.
Um, I was working...
FLAP!
FIREWORKS BY RUGGIERI
STARS AND EFFECTS
TIME FUSE
PROPELLANT
HOLLOW CORE
FUSE
The oxidizer and the fuel are mixed with a binding material. We call the mixture ***the grain.***
Nozzle wear isn't a concern with nonreusable rockets like fireworks.
But the American space shuttle used reusable solid-propellant boosters to get into space.
SOLID BOOSTER
SOLID BOOSTER
The nozzle is sometimes covered with an ***ablative material*** like the heat shield on the shuttle's bottom.
What's with the hollow core in the fireworks, though?
The core and its shape affect the burn rate, giving different thrusts!

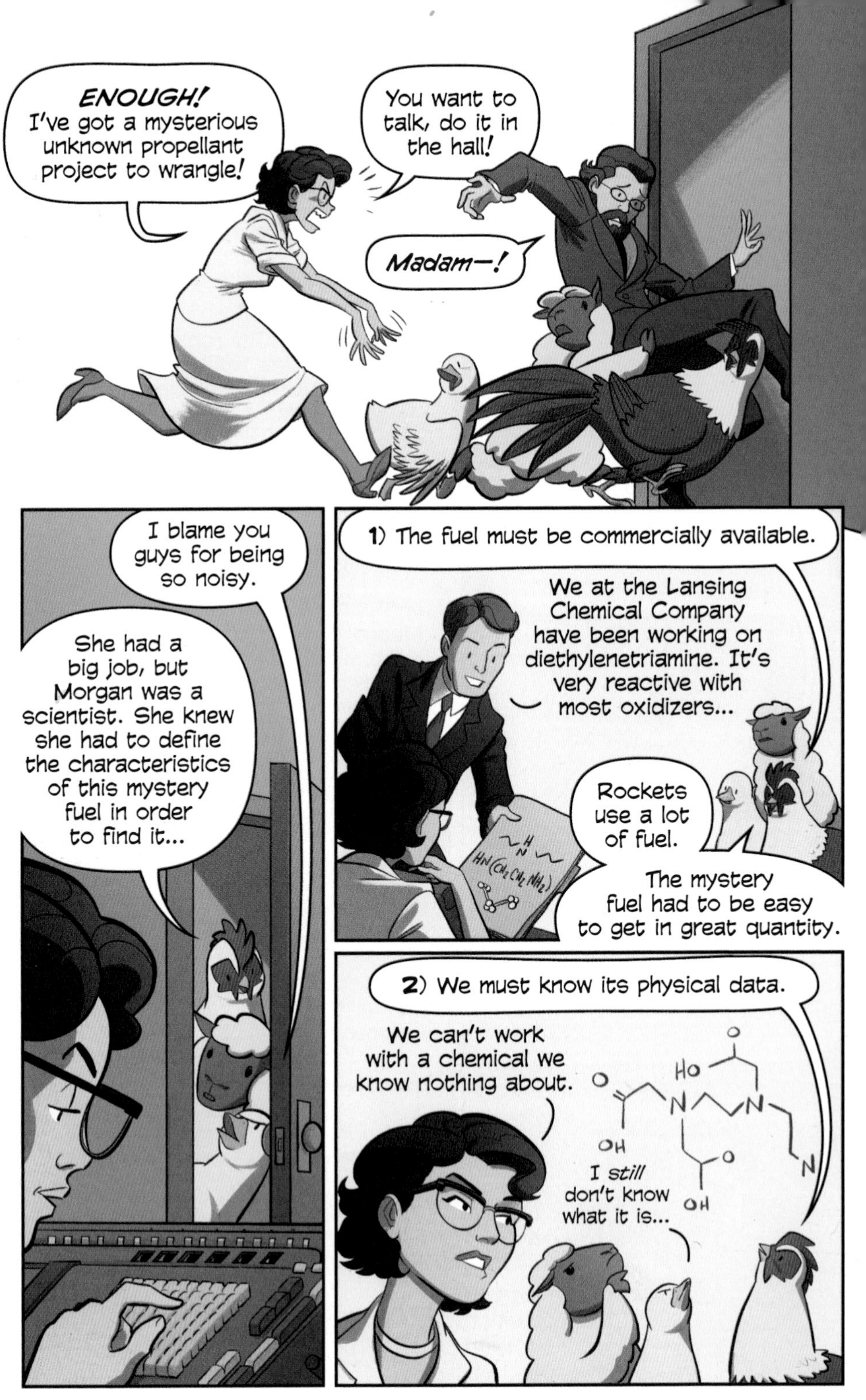
ENOUGH! I've got a mysterious unknown propellant project to wrangle!
You want to talk, do it in the hall!
Madam—!
I blame you guys for being so noisy.
She had a big job, but Morgan was a scientist. She knew she had to define the characteristics of this mystery fuel in order to find it...
1) The fuel must be commercially available.
We at the Lansing Chemical Company have been working on diethylenetriamine. It's very reactive with most oxidizers...
HN(CH2CH2NH2)
Rockets use a lot of fuel.
The mystery fuel had to be easy to get in great quantity.
2) We must know its physical data.
We can't work with a chemical we know nothing about.
I still don't know what it is...

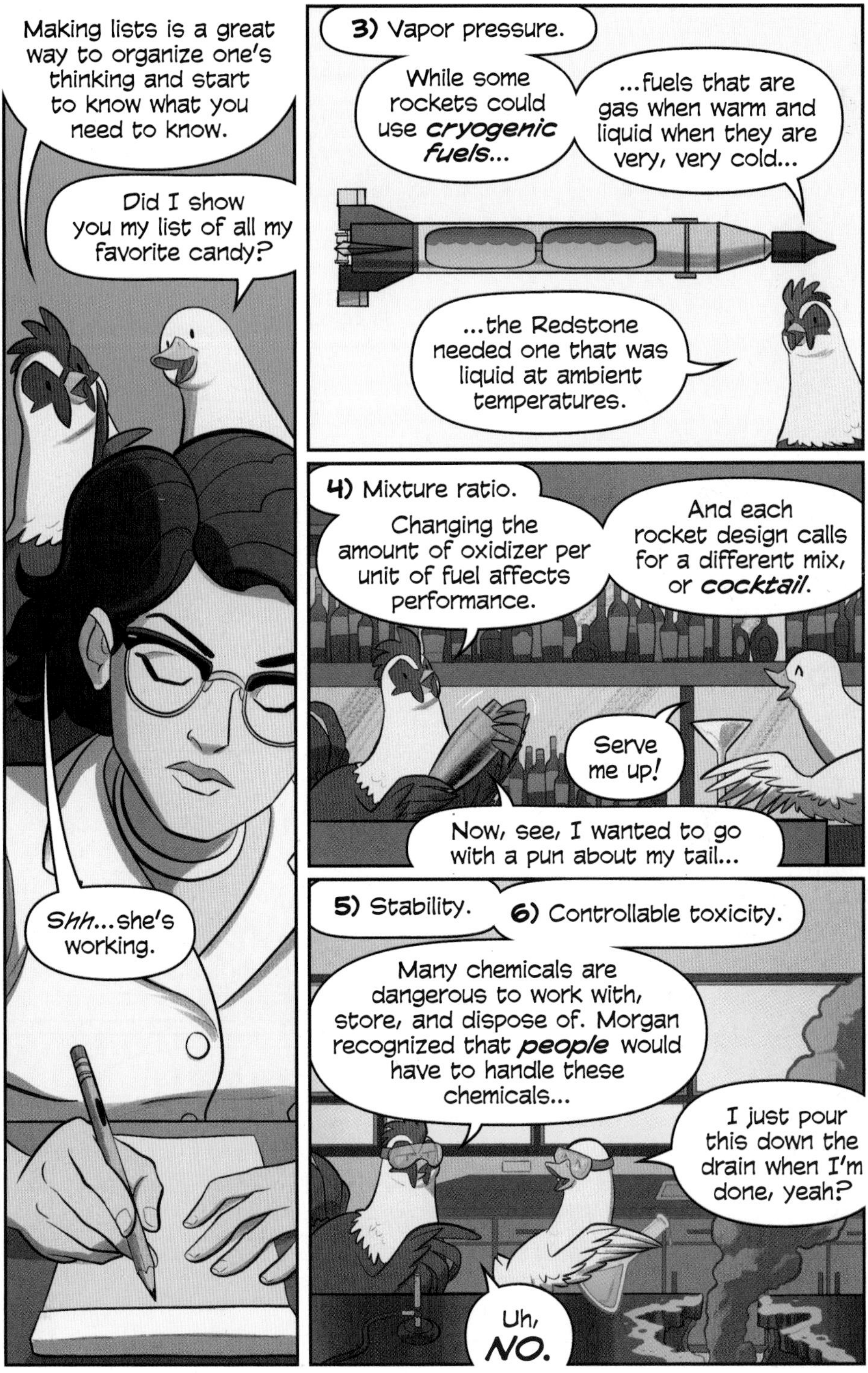

Making lists is a great way to organize one's thinking and start to know what you need to know.
Did I show you my list of all my favorite candy?
Shh...she's working.
3) Vapor pressure.
While some rockets could use *cryogenic fuels*...
...fuels that are gas when warm and liquid when they are very, very cold...
...the Redstone needed one that was liquid at ambient temperatures.
4) Mixture ratio.
Changing the amount of oxidizer per unit of fuel affects performance.
And each rocket design calls for a different mix, or *cocktail*.
Serve me up!
Now, see, I wanted to go with a pun about my tail...
5) Stability.
6) Controllable toxicity.
Many chemicals are dangerous to work with, store, and dispose of. Morgan recognized that *people* would have to handle these chemicals...
I just pour this down the drain when I'm done, yeah?
Uh, *NO.*

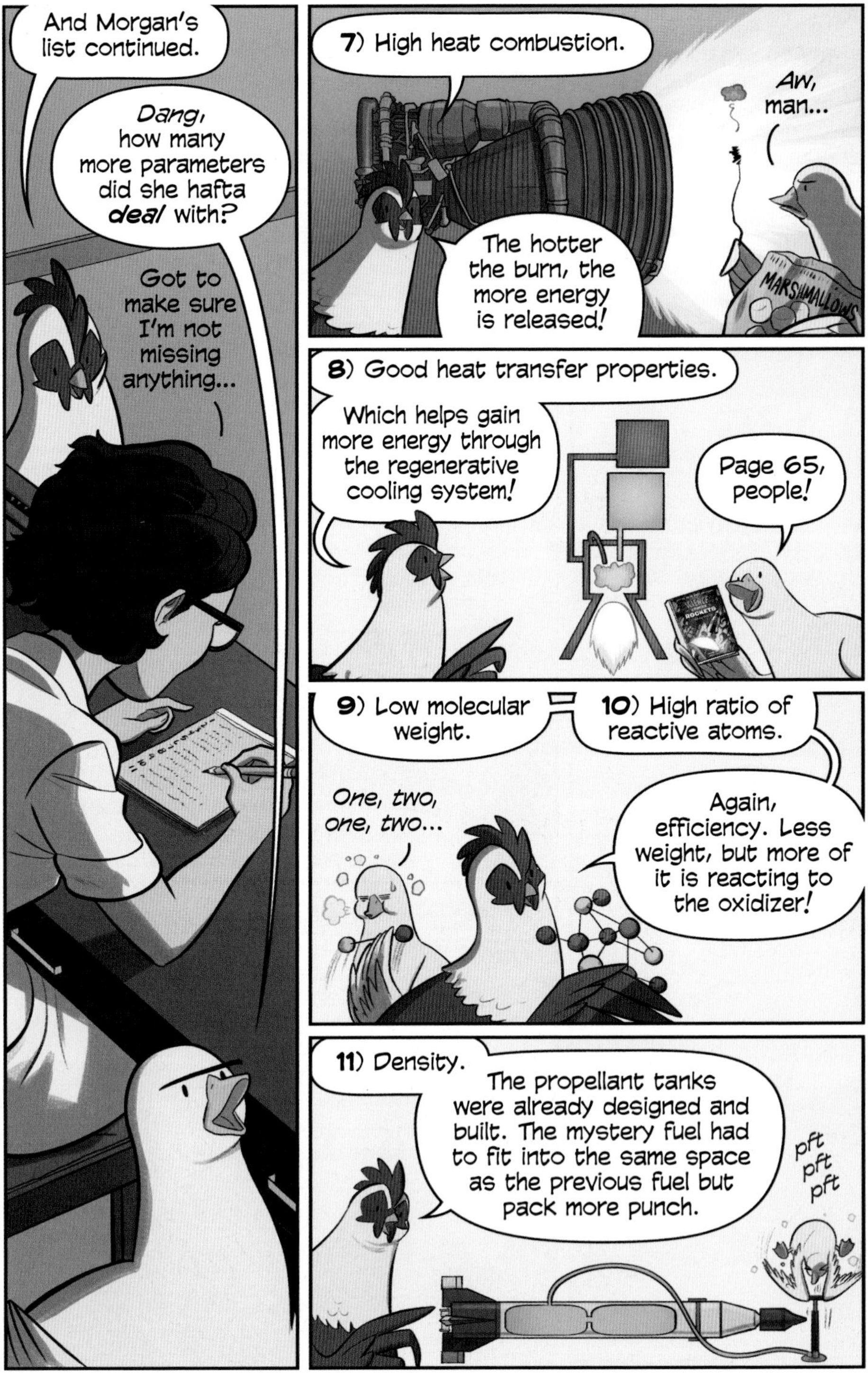
And Morgan's list continued.
Dang, how many more parameters did she hafta ***deal*** with?
Got to make sure I'm not missing anything...
7) High heat combustion.
Aw, man...
The hotter the burn, the more energy is released!
MARSHMALLOWS
8) Good heat transfer properties.
Which helps gain more energy through the regenerative cooling system!
Page 65, people!
9) Low molecular weight.
10) High ratio of reactive atoms.
One, two, one, two...
Again, efficiency. Less weight, but more of it is reacting to the oxidizer!
11) Density.
The propellant tanks were already designed and built. The mystery fuel had to fit into the same space as the previous fuel but pack more punch.
pft pft pft

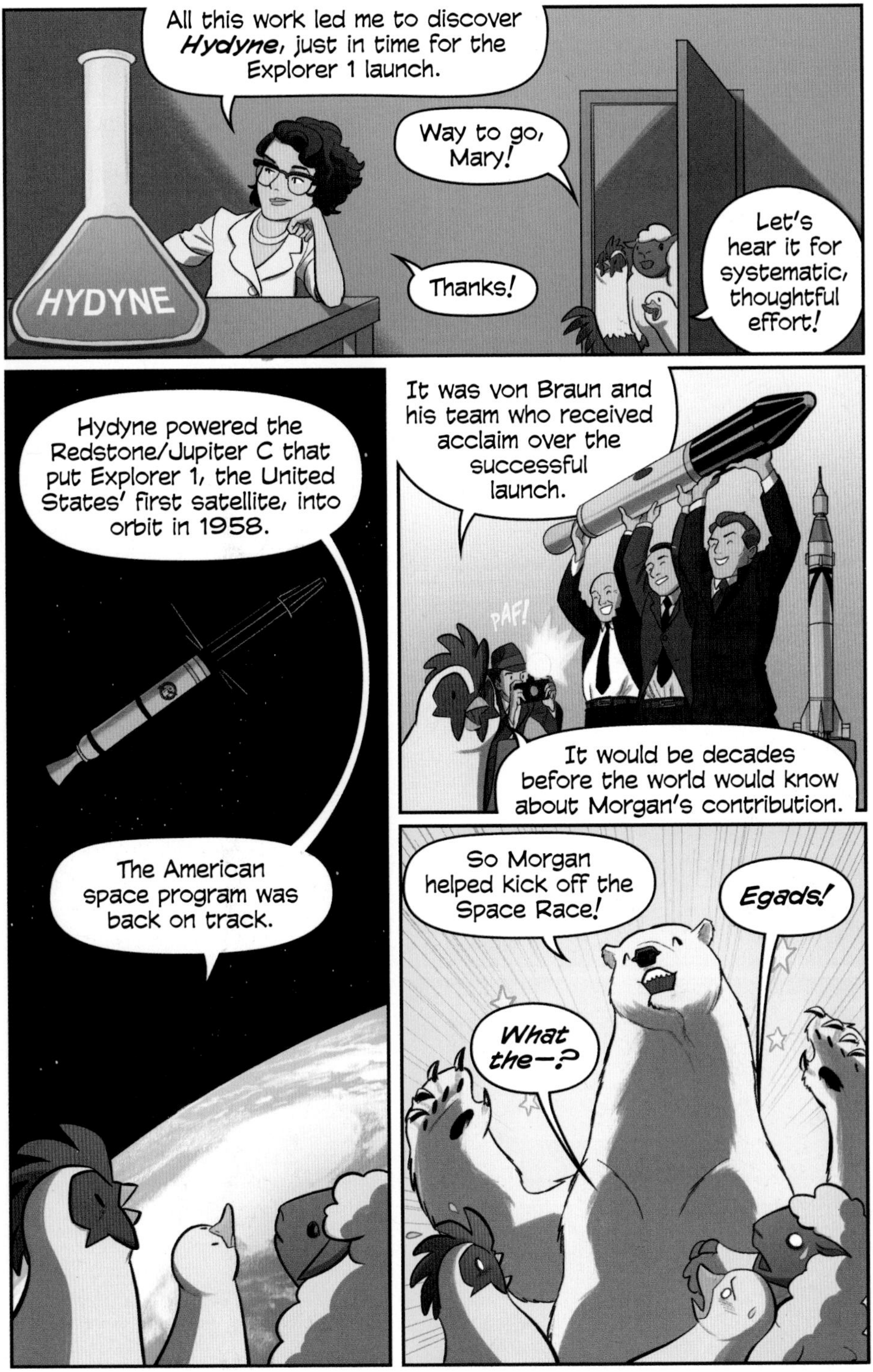
All this work led me to discover *Hydyne*, just in time for the Explorer 1 launch.
Way to go, Mary!
Let's hear it for systematic, thoughtful effort!
Thanks!
HYDYNE
Hydyne powered the Redstone/Jupiter C that put Explorer 1, the United States' first satellite, into orbit in 1958.
It was von Braun and his team who received acclaim over the successful launch.
PAF!
It would be decades before the world would know about Morgan's contribution.
The American space program was back on track.
So Morgan helped kick off the Space Race!
Egads!
What the—?

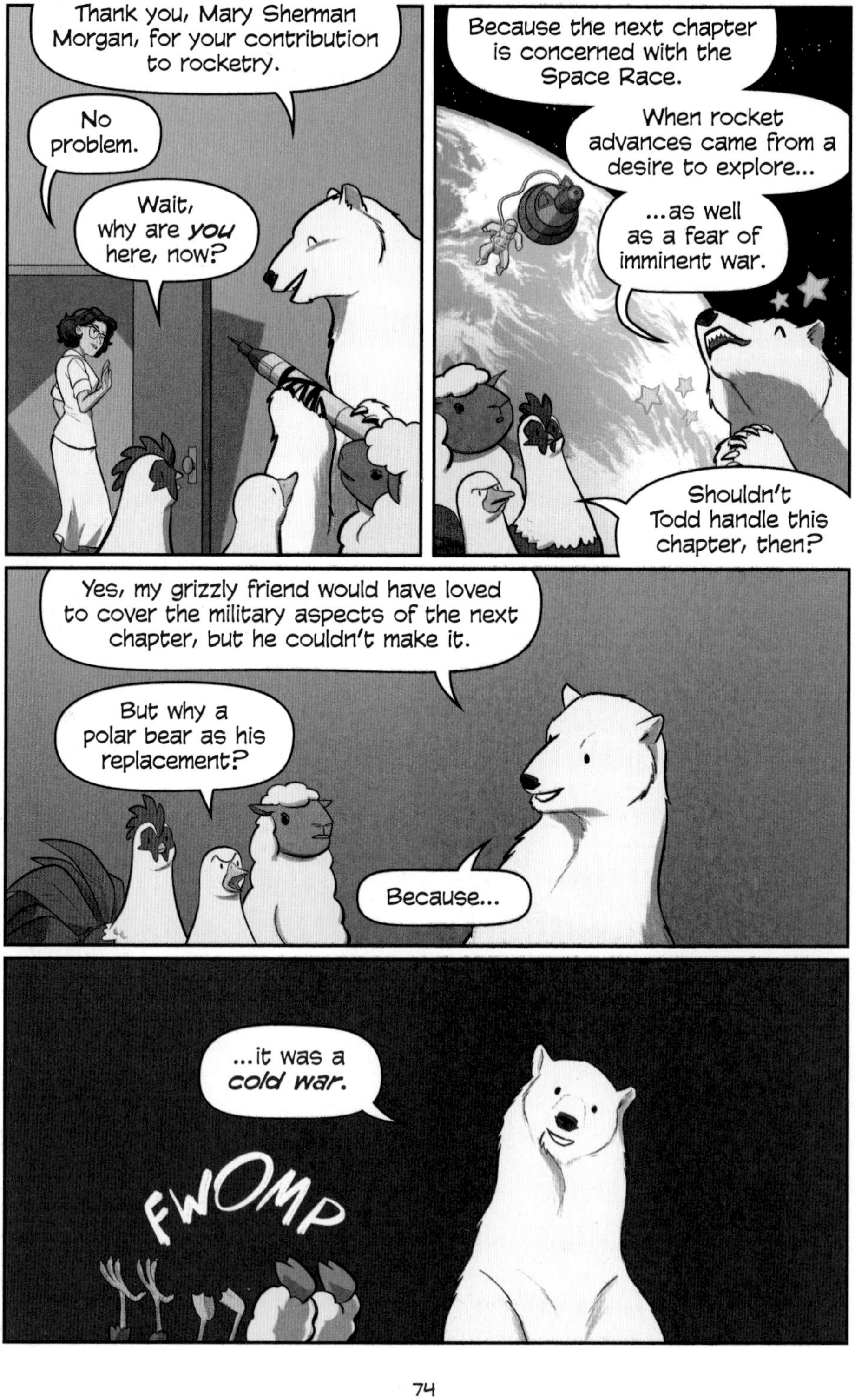
Thank you, Mary Sherman Morgan, for your contribution to rocketry.
No problem.
Wait, why are *you* here, now?
Because the next chapter is concerned with the Space Race.
When rocket advances came from a desire to explore...
...as well as a fear of imminent war.
Shouldn't Todd handle this chapter, then?
Yes, my grizzly friend would have loved to cover the military aspects of the next chapter, but he couldn't make it.
But why a polar bear as his replacement?
Because...
...it was a *cold war.*
FWOMP

CHAPTER 5: ROCKETS IN THE SPACE RACE

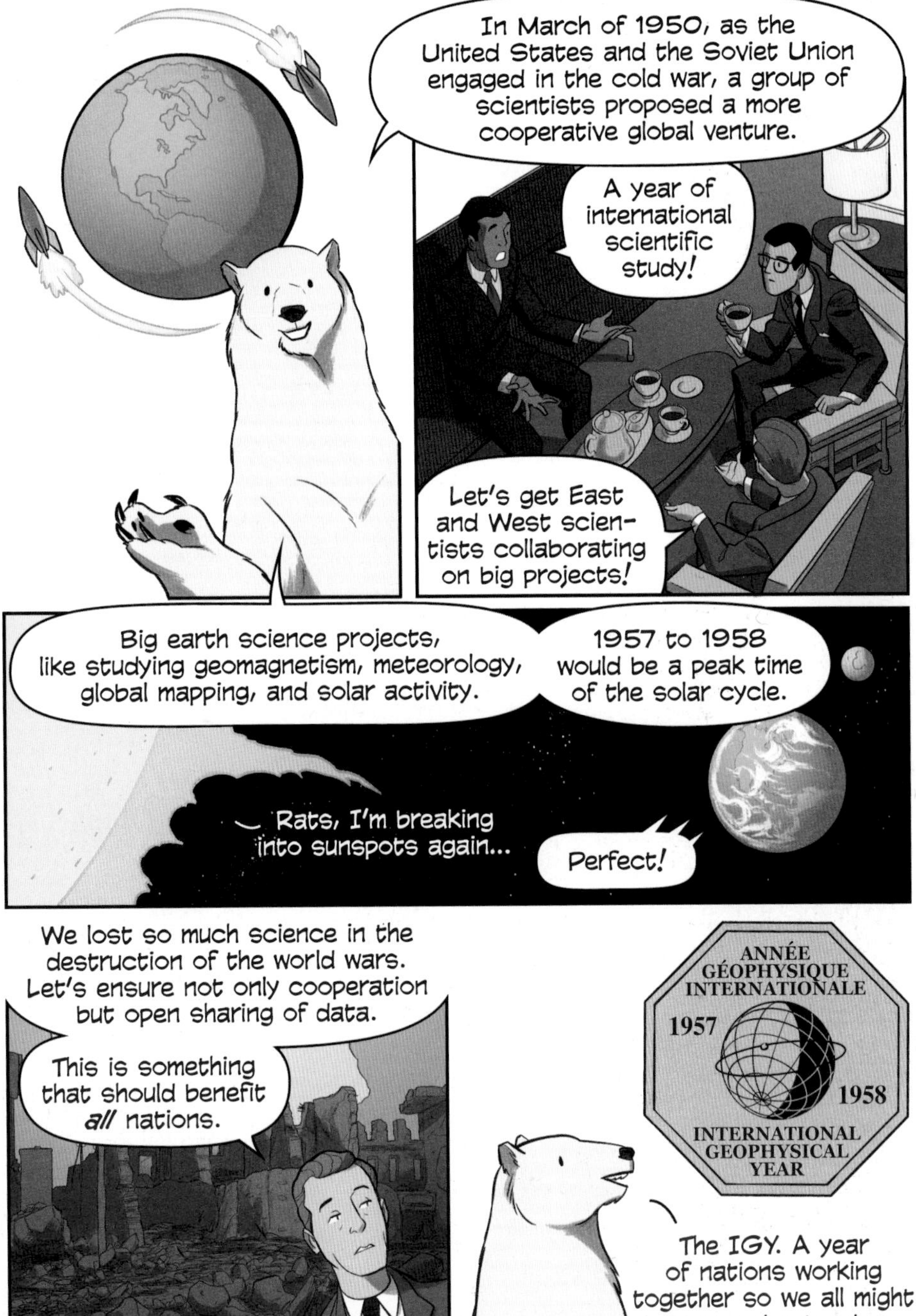
In March of 1950, as the United States and the Soviet Union engaged in the cold war, a group of scientists proposed a more cooperative global venture.
A year of international scientific study!
Let's get East and West scien-tists collaborating on big projects!
Big earth science projects, like studying geomagnetism, meteorology, global mapping, and solar activity.
1957 to 1958 would be a peak time of the solar cycle.
Rats, I'm breaking into sunspots again...
Perfect!
We lost so much science in the destruction of the world wars. Let's ensure not only cooperation but open sharing of data.
This is something that should benefit *all* nations.
ANNÉE GÉOPHYSIQUE INTERNATIONALE
1957
1958
INTERNATIONAL GEOPHYSICAL YEAR
The IGY. A year of nations working together so we all might better understand our planet. Cool, huh?

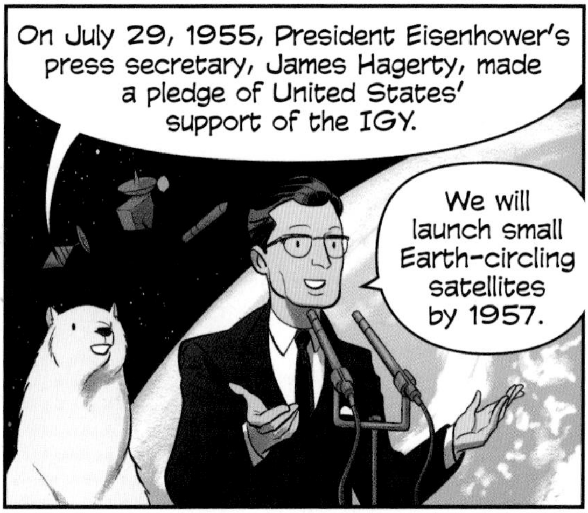
On July 29, 1955, President Eisenhower's press secretary, James Hagerty, made a pledge of United States' support of the IGY.
We will launch small Earth-circling satellites by 1957.

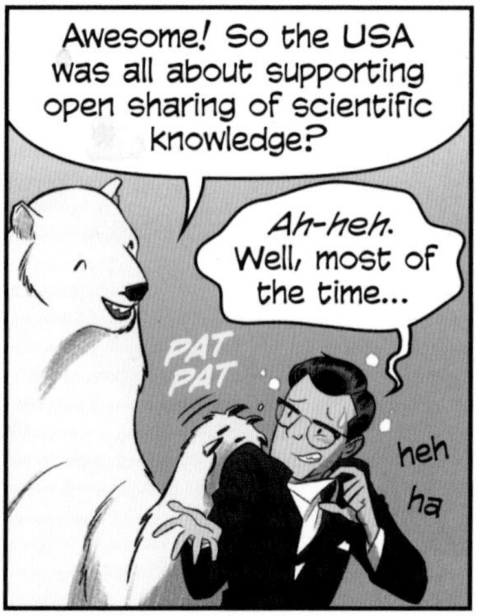
Awesome! So the USA was all about supporting open sharing of scientific knowledge?
Ah-heh. Well, most of the time...
PAT PAT
heh
ha

1945: OPERATION PAPERCLIP

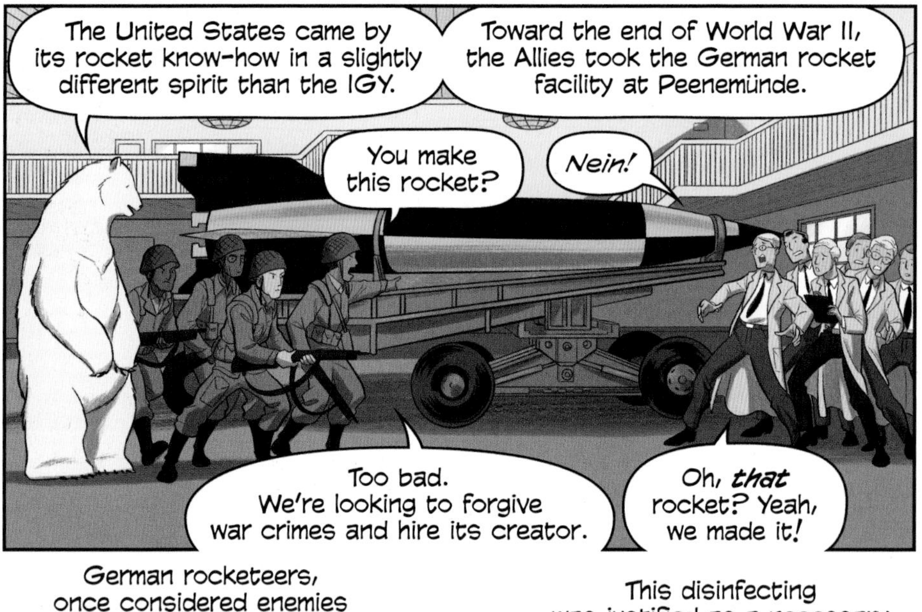
The United States came by its rocket know-how in a slightly different spirit than the IGY.
Toward the end of World War II, the Allies took the German rocket facility at Peenemünde.
You make this rocket?
Nein!
Too bad. We're looking to forgive war crimes and hire its creator.
Oh, ***that*** rocket? Yeah, we made it!

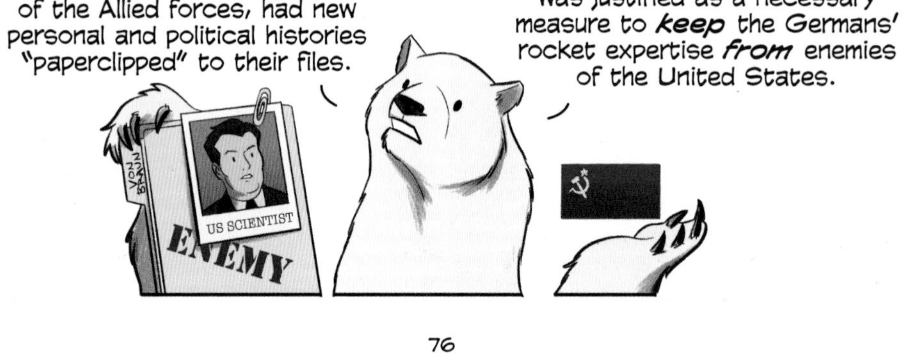
German rocketeers, once considered enemies of the Allied forces, had new personal and political histories "paperclipped" to their files.
This disinfecting was justified as a necessary measure to ***keep*** the Germans' rocket expertise ***from*** enemies of the United States.
VON BRAUN
US SCIENTIST
ENEMY

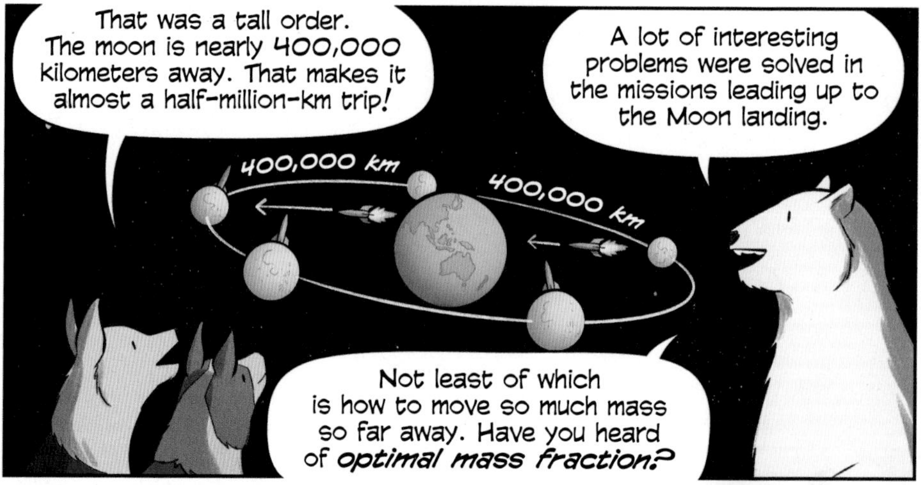

That was a tall order. The moon is nearly 400,000 kilometers away. That makes it almost a half-million-km trip!
A lot of interesting problems were solved in the missions leading up to the Moon landing.
400,000 km
400,000 km
Not least of which is how to move so much mass so far away. Have you heard of *optimal mass fraction?*

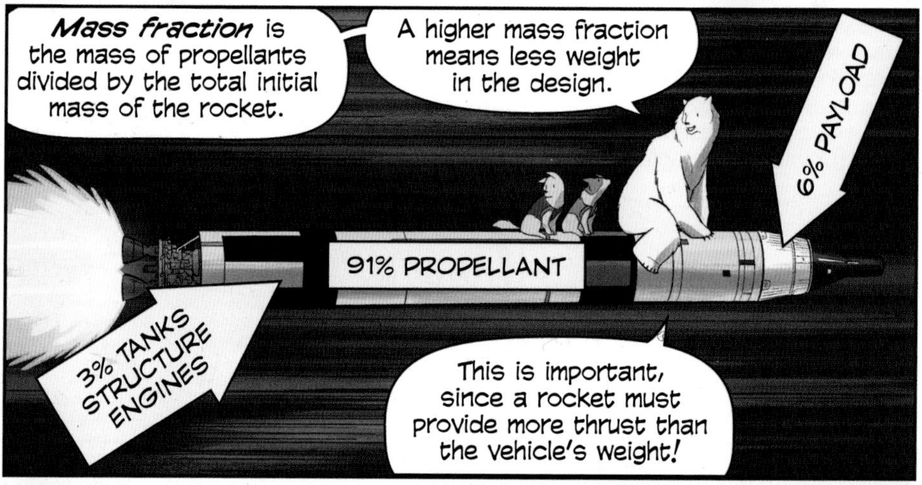

Mass fraction is the mass of propellants divided by the total initial mass of the rocket.
A higher mass fraction means less weight in the design.
6% PAYLOAD
91% PROPELLANT
3% TANKS STRUCTURE ENGINES
This is important, since a rocket must provide more thrust than the vehicle's weight!

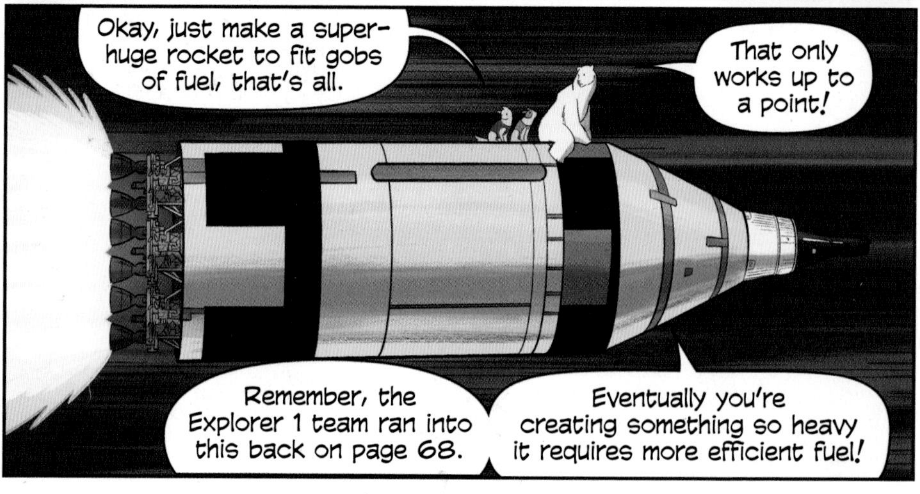

Okay, just make a super-huge rocket to fit gobs of fuel, that's all.
That only works up to a point!
Remember, the Explorer 1 team ran into this back on page 68.
Eventually you're creating something so heavy it requires more efficient fuel!

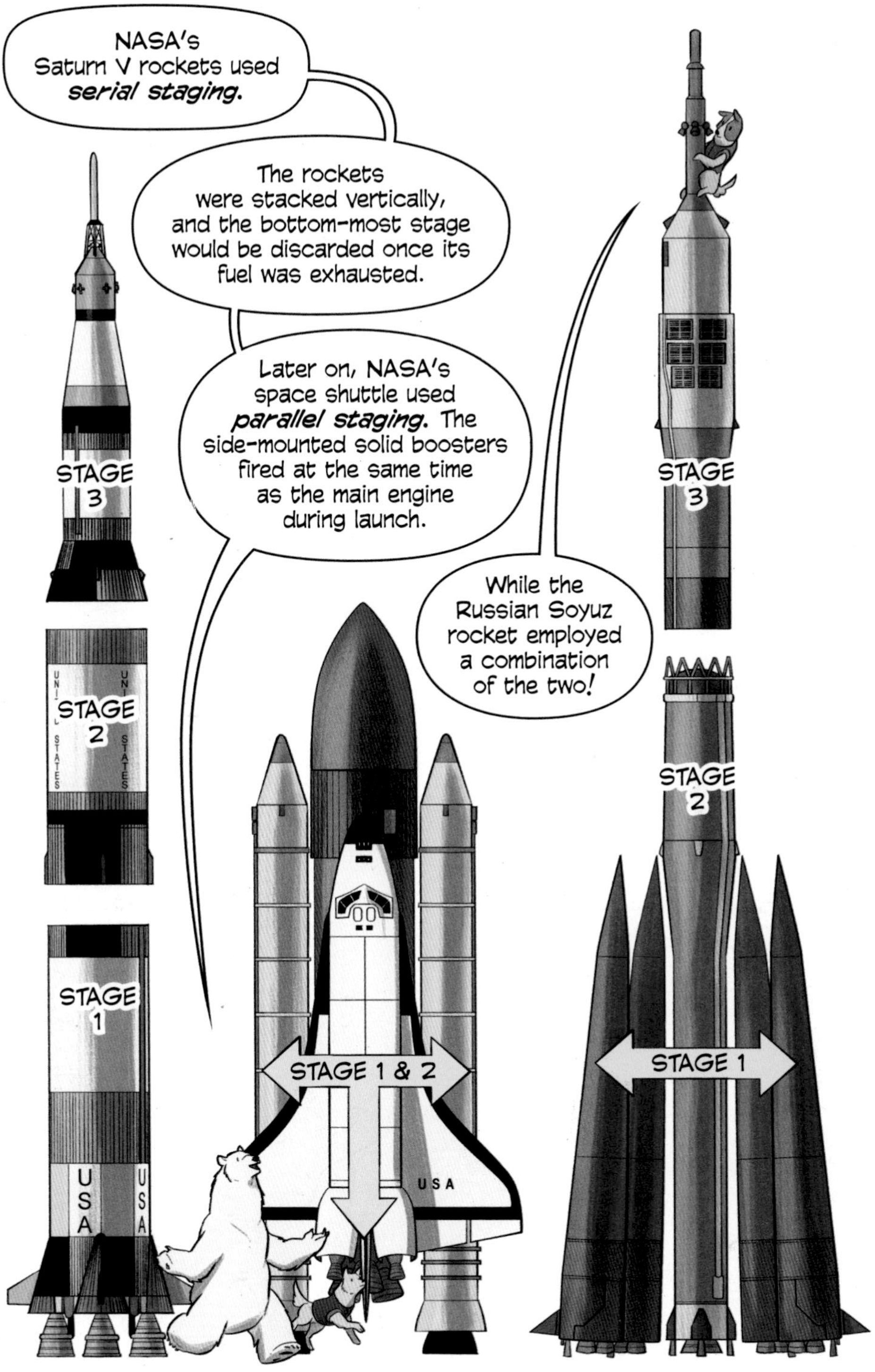
NASA's Saturn V rockets used ***serial staging***.
The rockets were stacked vertically, and the bottom-most stage would be discarded once its fuel was exhausted.
Later on, NASA's space shuttle used ***parallel staging***. The side-mounted solid boosters fired at the same time as the main engine during launch.
While the Russian Soyuz rocket employed a combination of the two!
STAGE 3
STAGE 2
STAGE 1
USA
STAGE 1 & 2
USA
STAGE 3
STAGE 2
STAGE 1

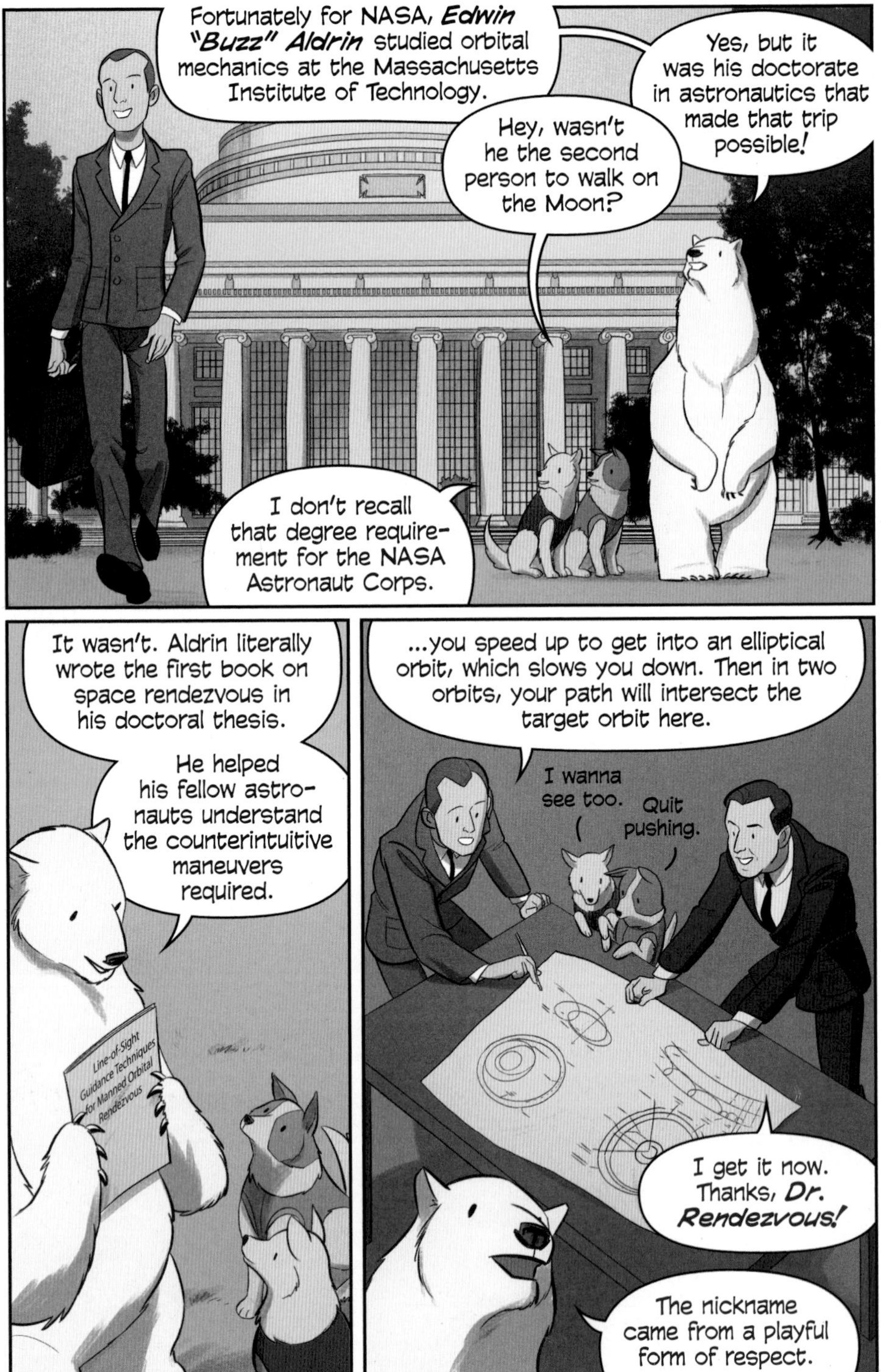
Fortunately for NASA, ***Edwin "Buzz" Aldrin*** studied orbital mechanics at the Massachusetts Institute of Technology.
Yes, but it was his doctorate in astronautics that made that trip possible!
Hey, wasn't he the second person to walk on the Moon?
I don't recall that degree requirement for the NASA Astronaut Corps.
It wasn't. Aldrin literally wrote the first book on space rendezvous in his doctoral thesis.
He helped his fellow astronauts understand the counterintuitive maneuvers required.
Line-of-Sight Guidance Techniques for Manned Orbital Rendezvous
...you speed up to get into an elliptical orbit, which slows you down. Then in two orbits, your path will intersect the target orbit here.
I wanna see too.
Quit pushing.
I get it now. Thanks, ***Dr. Rendezvous!***
The nickname came from a playful form of respect.

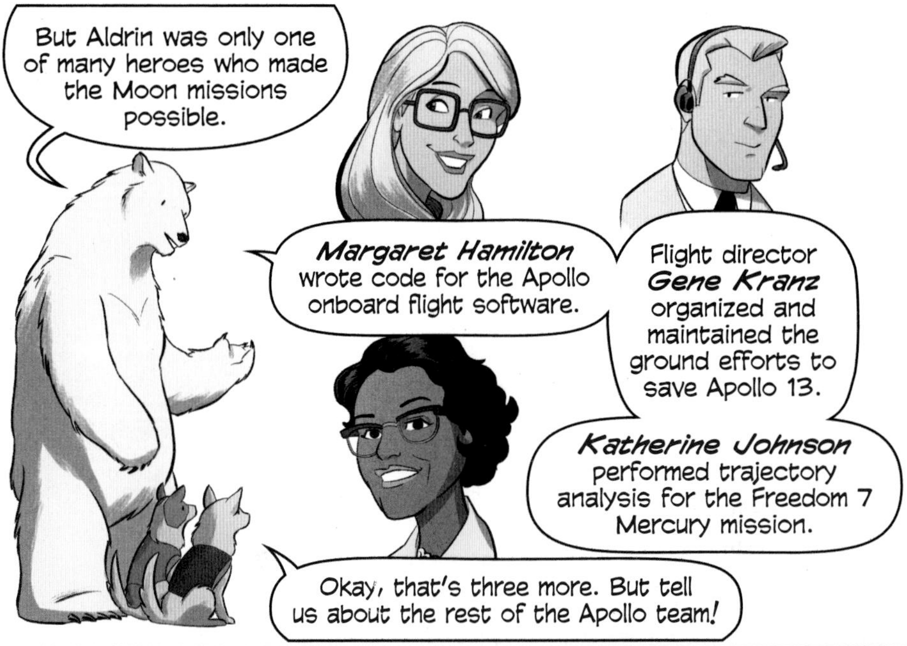
But Aldrin was only one of many heroes who made the Moon missions possible.
Margaret Hamilton wrote code for the Apollo onboard flight software.
Flight director Gene Kranz organized and maintained the ground efforts to save Apollo 13.
Katherine Johnson performed trajectory analysis for the Freedom 7 Mercury mission.
Okay, that's three more. But tell us about the rest of the Apollo team!

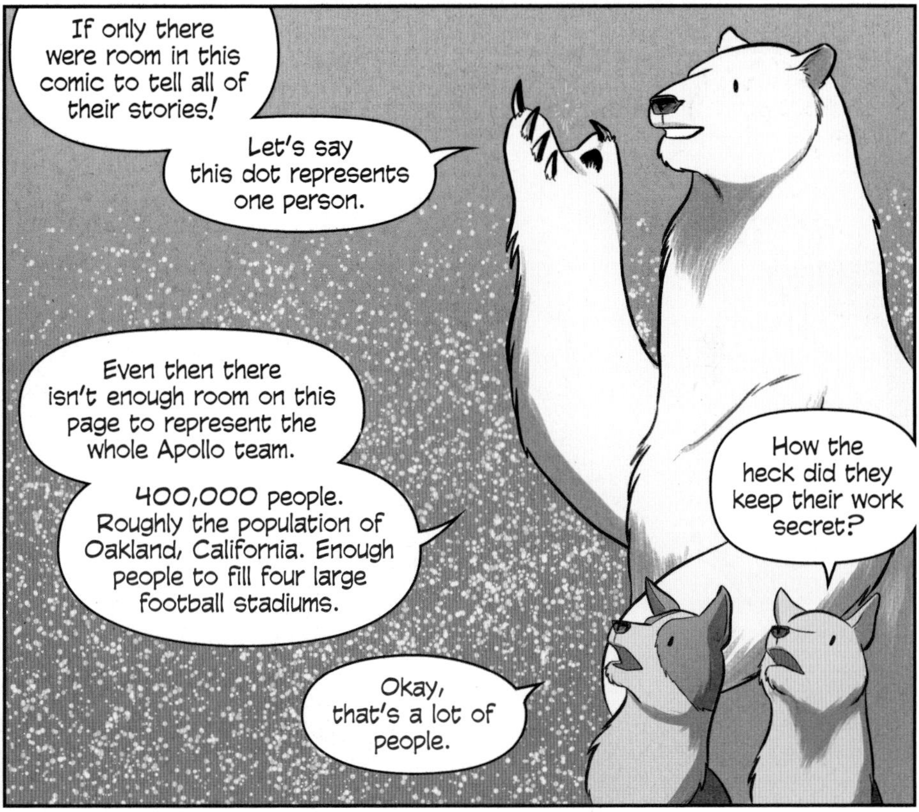
If only there were room in this comic to tell all of their stories!
Let's say this dot represents one person.
Even then there isn't enough room on this page to represent the whole Apollo team.
400,000 people. Roughly the population of Oakland, California. Enough people to fill four large football stadiums.
How the heck did they keep their work secret?
Okay, that's a lot of people.

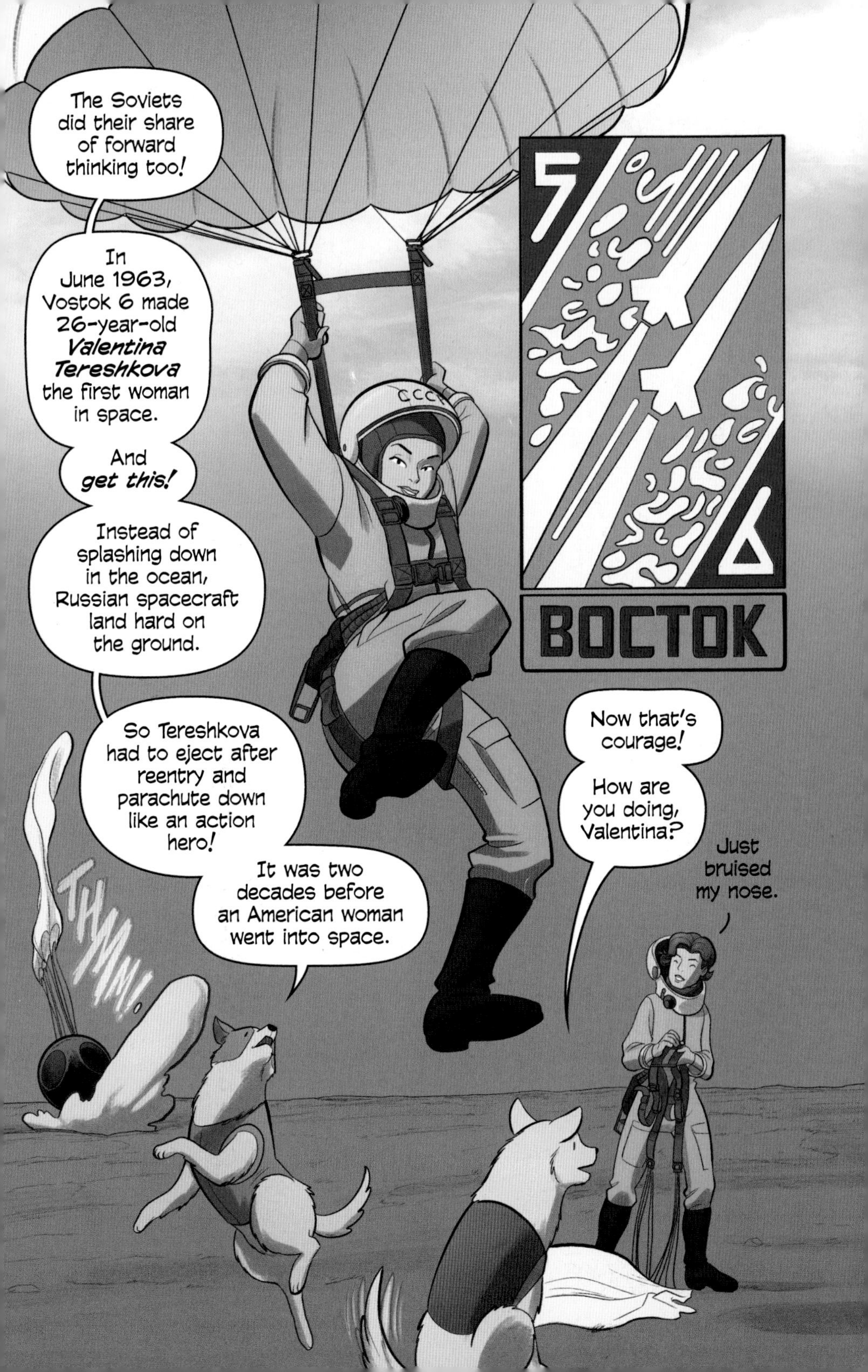
The Soviets did their share of forward thinking too!
In June 1963, Vostok 6 made 26-year-old *Valentina Tereshkova* the first woman in space.
And *get this!*
Instead of splashing down in the ocean, Russian spacecraft land hard on the ground.
So Tereshkova had to eject after reentry and parachute down like an action hero!
It was two decades before an American woman went into space.
5
6
ВОСТОК
CCCP
THMM!
Now that's courage!
How are you doing, Valentina?
Just bruised my nose.

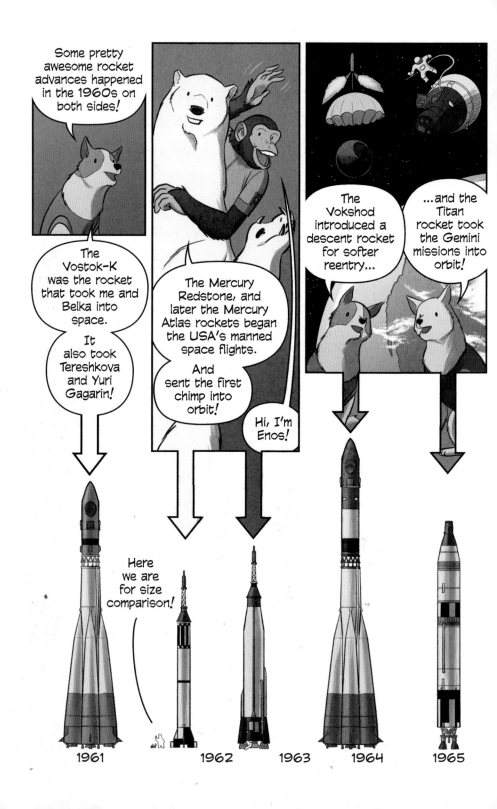

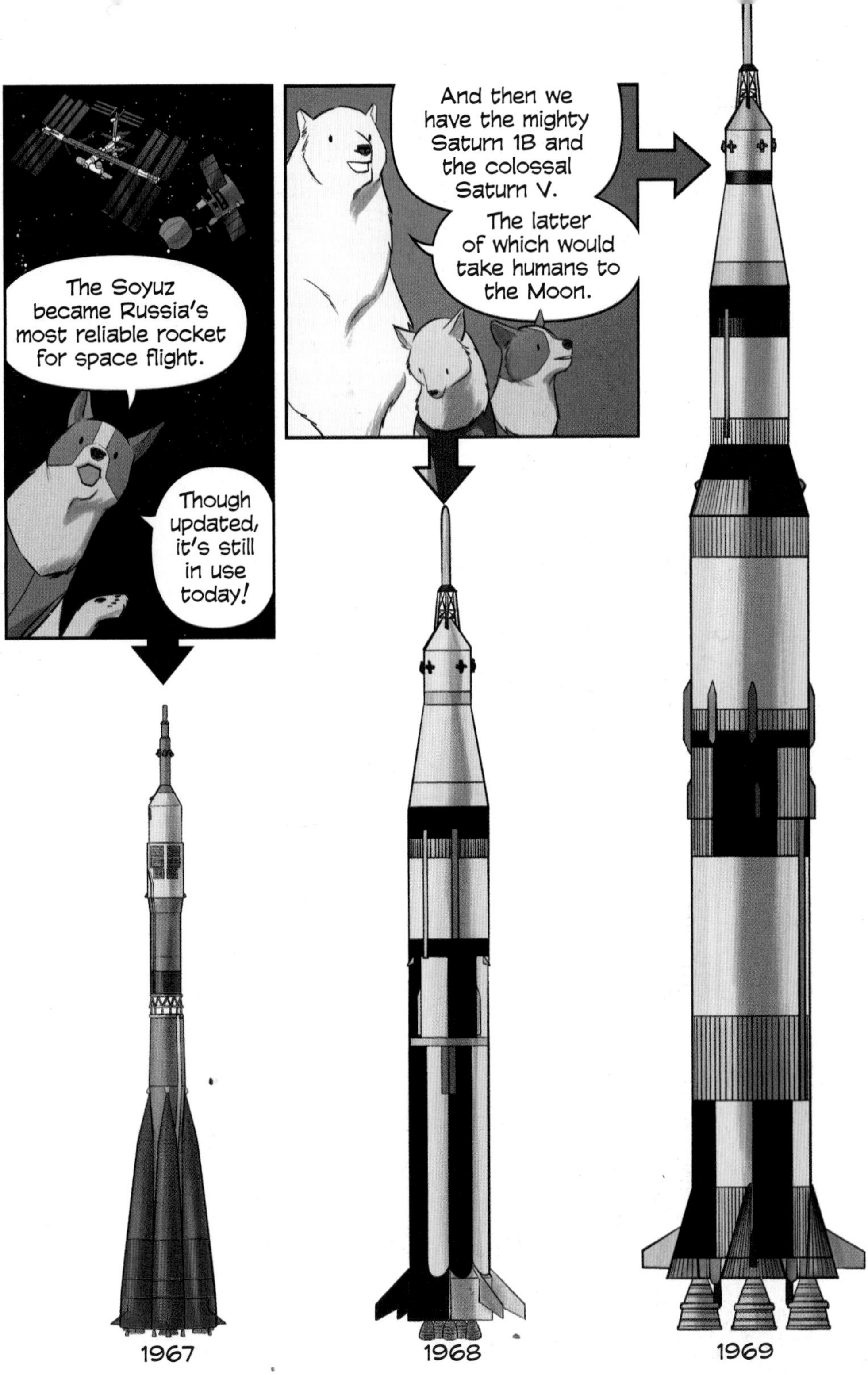
The Soyuz became Russia's most reliable rocket for space flight.
Though updated, it's still in use today!
And then we have the mighty Saturn 1B and the colossal Saturn V.
The latter of which would take humans to the Moon.
1967
1968
1969

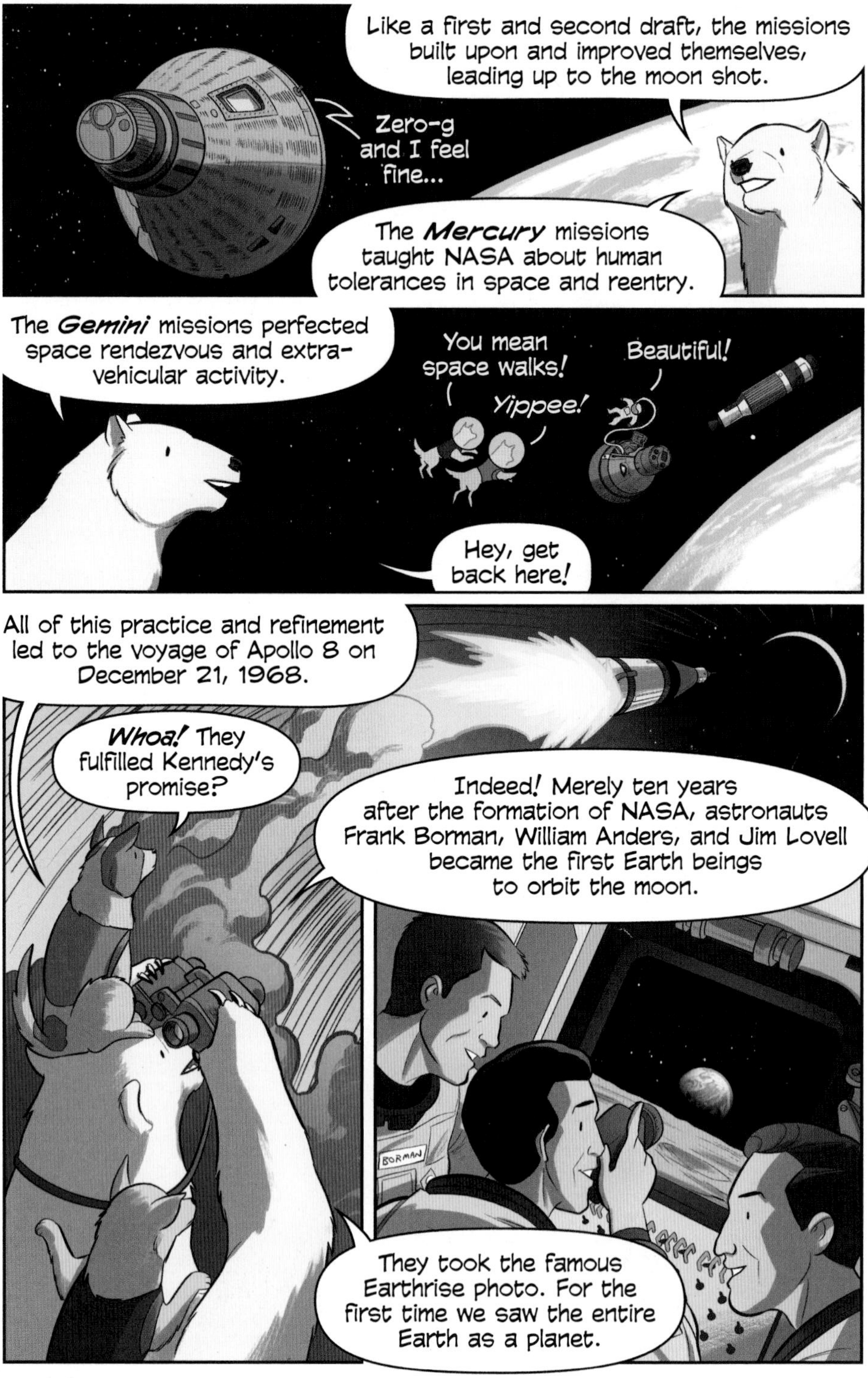
Like a first and second draft, the missions built upon and improved themselves, leading up to the moon shot.
Zero-g and I feel fine...
The *Mercury* missions taught NASA about human tolerances in space and reentry.
The *Gemini* missions perfected space rendezvous and extra-vehicular activity.
You mean space walks!
Yippee!
Beautiful!
Hey, get back here!
All of this practice and refinement led to the voyage of Apollo 8 on December 21, 1968.
Whoa! They fulfilled Kennedy's promise?
Indeed! Merely ten years after the formation of NASA, astronauts Frank Borman, William Anders, and Jim Lovell became the first Earth beings to orbit the moon.
BORMAN
They took the famous Earthrise photo. For the first time we saw the entire Earth as a planet.

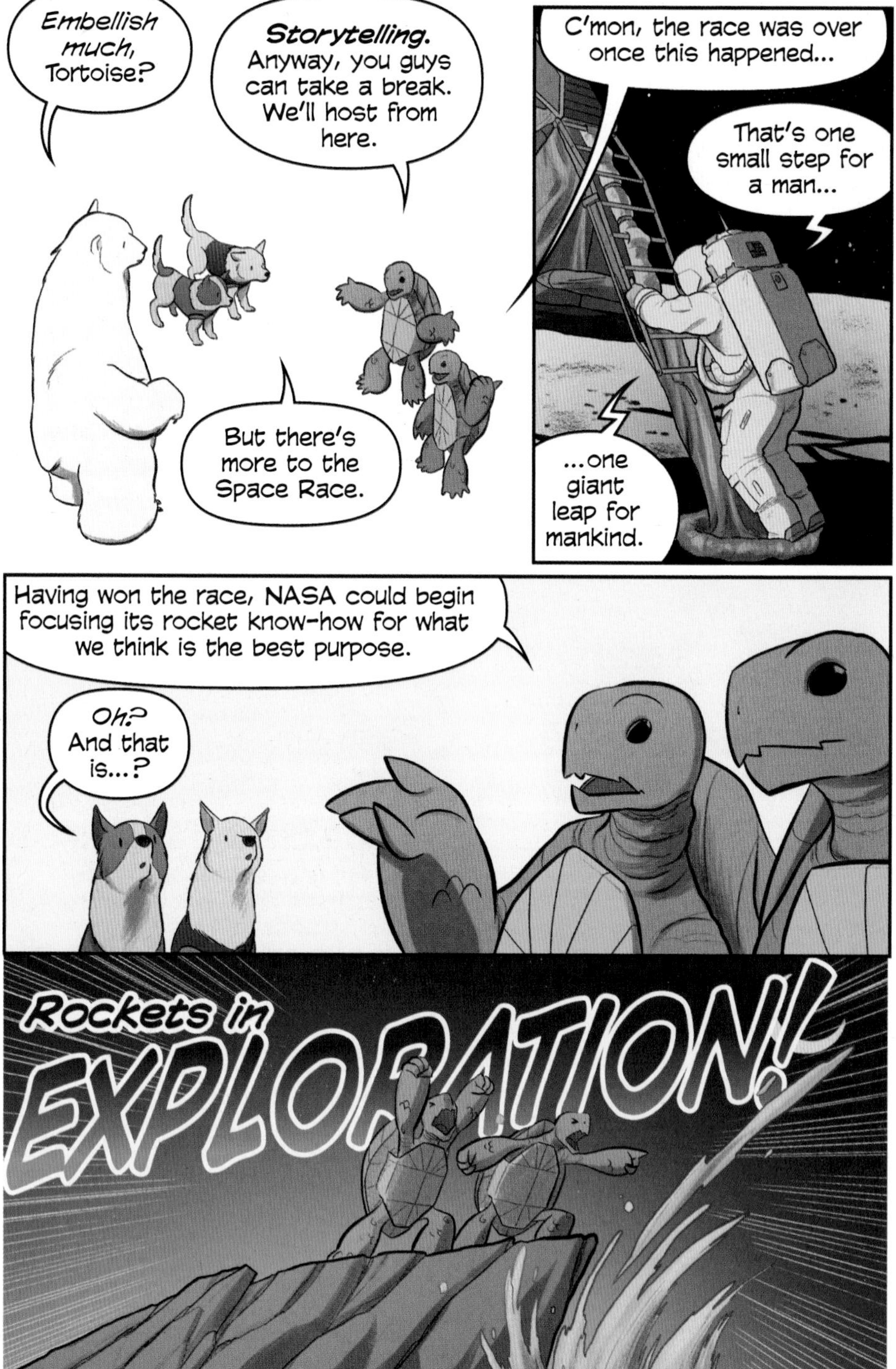
Embellish much, Tortoise?
Storytelling. Anyway, you guys can take a break. We'll host from here.
But there's more to the Space Race.
C'mon, the race was over once this happened...
That's one small step for a man...
...one giant leap for mankind.
Having won the race, NASA could begin focusing its rocket know-how for what we think is the best purpose.
Oh? And that is...?
Rockets in EXPLORATION!

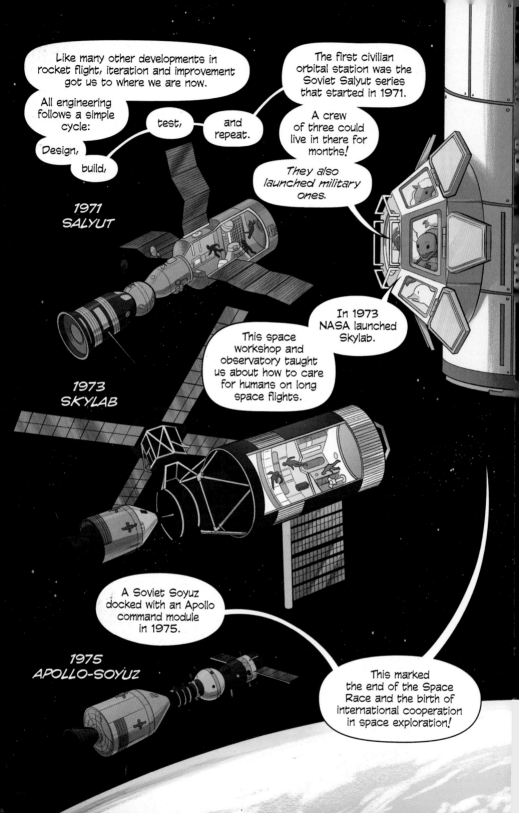

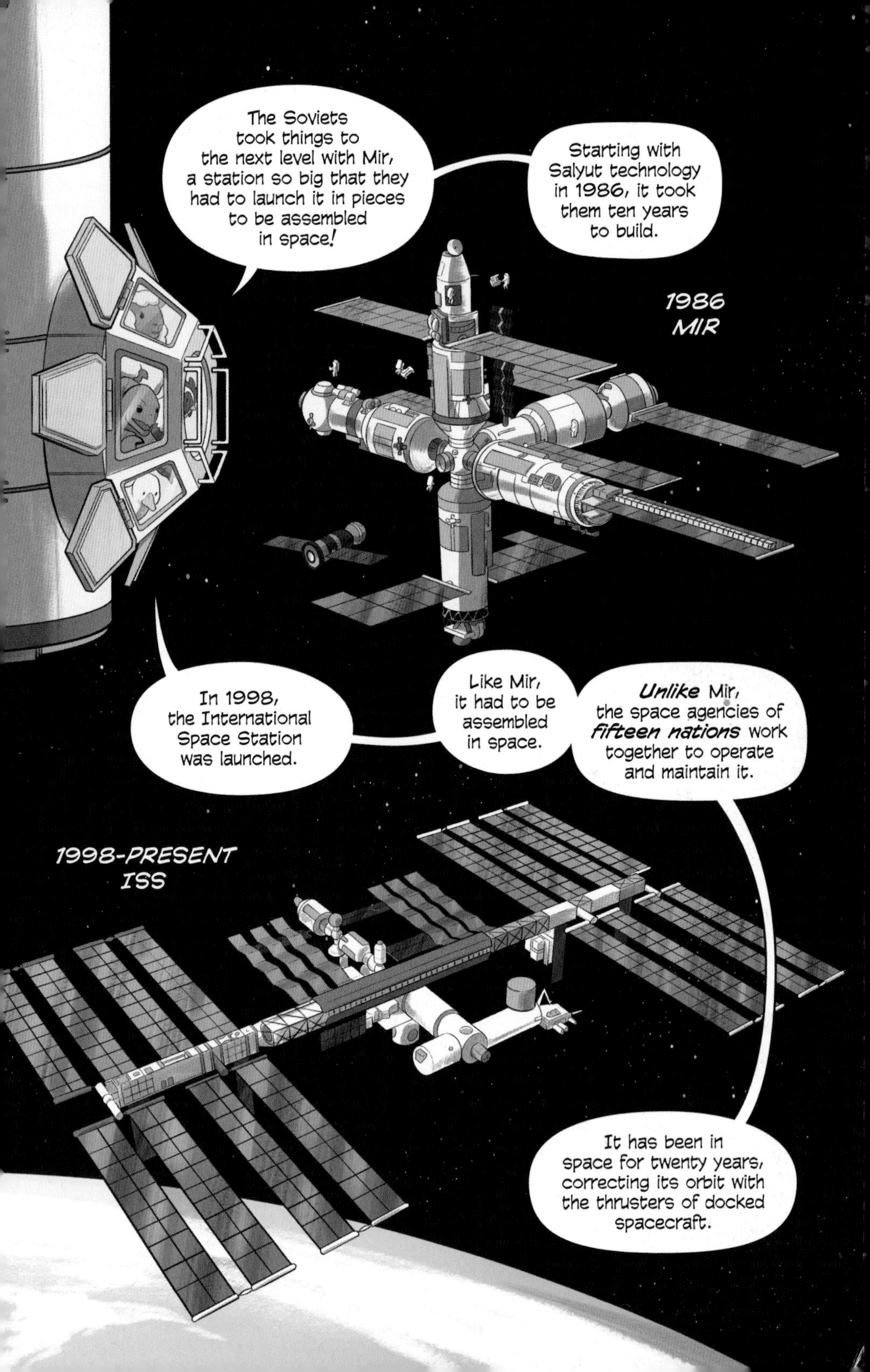
The Soviets took things to the next level with Mir, a station so big that they had to launch it in pieces to be assembled in space!
Starting with Salyut technology in 1986, it took them ten years to build.
1986 MIR
In 1998, the International Space Station was launched.
Like Mir, it had to be assembled in space.
Unlike Mir, the space agencies of ***fifteen nations*** work together to operate and maintain it.
1998-PRESENT ISS
It has been in space for twenty years, correcting its orbit with the thrusters of docked spacecraft.

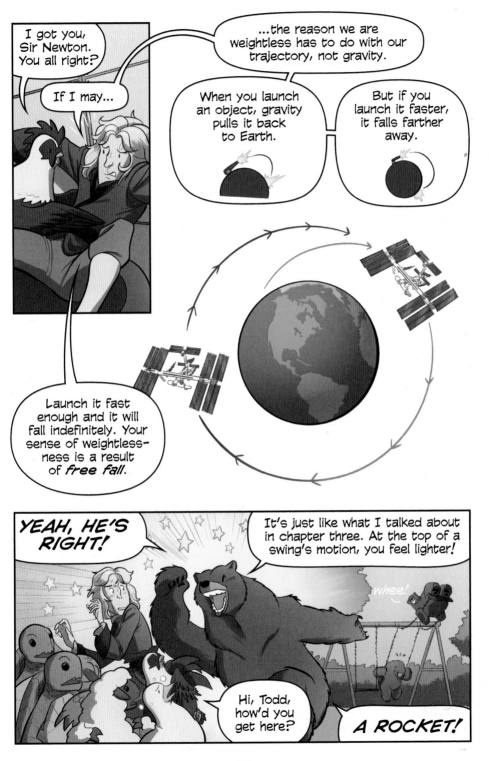

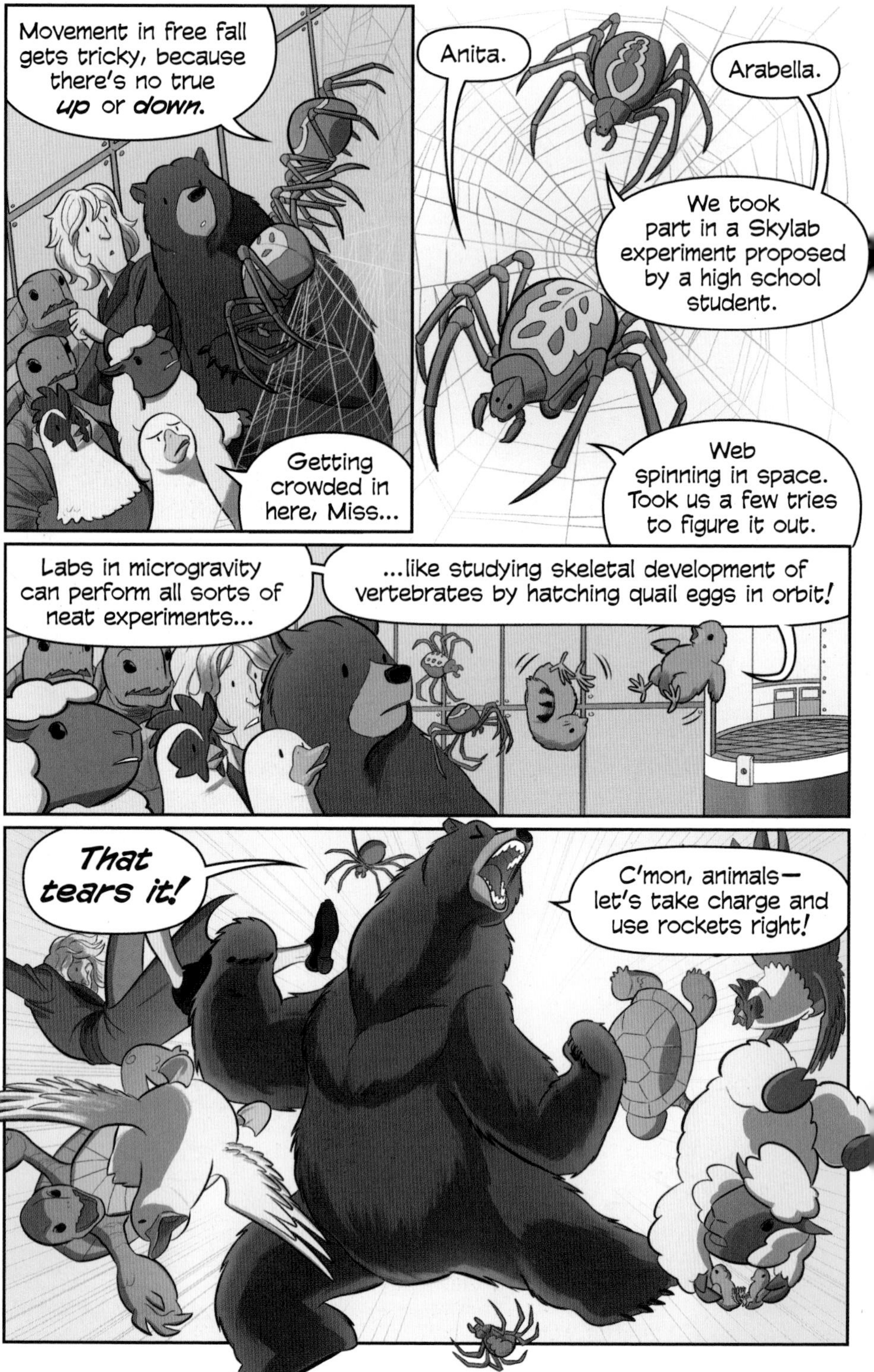
Movement in free fall gets tricky, because there's no true *up* or *down*.
Getting crowded in here, Miss...
Anita.
Arabella.
We took part in a Skylab experiment proposed by a high school student.
Web spinning in space. Took us a few tries to figure it out.
Labs in microgravity can perform all sorts of neat experiments...
...like studying skeletal development of vertebrates by hatching quail eggs in orbit!
That tears it!
C'mon, animals—let's take charge and use rockets right!

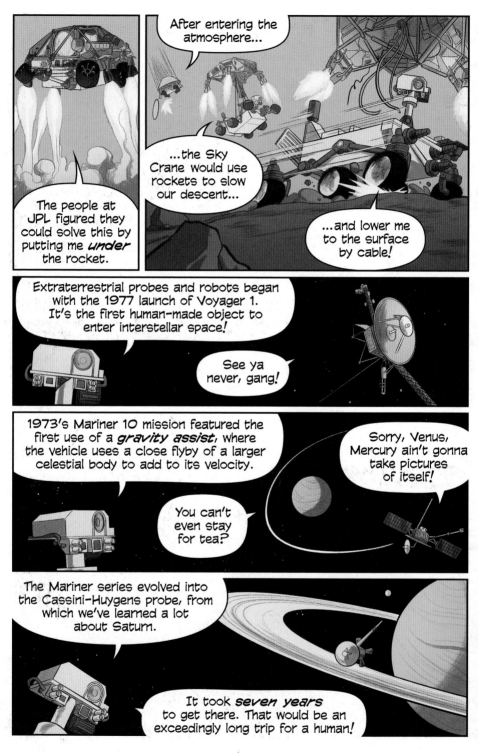

After entering the atmosphere...

The people at JPL figured they could solve this by putting me *under* the rocket.

...the Sky Crane would use rockets to slow our descent...

...and lower me to the surface by cable!

Extraterrestrial probes and robots began with the 1977 launch of Voyager 1. It's the first human-made object to enter interstellar space!

See ya never, gang!

1973's Mariner 10 mission featured the first use of a *gravity assist*, where the vehicle uses a close flyby of a larger celestial body to add to its velocity.

You can't even stay for tea?

Sorry, Venus, Mercury ain't gonna take pictures of itself!

The Mariner series evolved into the Cassini-Huygens probe, from which we've learned a lot about Saturn.

It took *seven years* to get there. That would be an exceedingly long trip for a human!

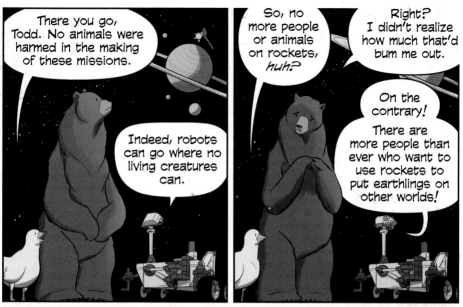

CHAPTER 7: THE FUTURE OF ROCKETS

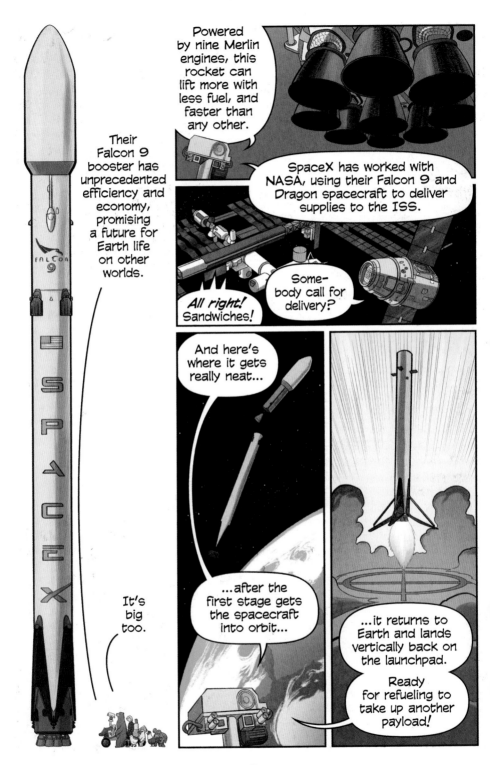

Their Falcon 9 booster has unprecedented efficiency and economy, promising a future for Earth life on other worlds.

It's big too.

Powered by nine Merlin engines, this rocket can lift more with less fuel, and faster than any other.

SpaceX has worked with NASA, using their Falcon 9 and Dragon spacecraft to deliver supplies to the ISS.

All right! Sandwiches!

Some-body call for delivery?

And here's where it gets really neat...

...after the first stage gets the spacecraft into orbit...

...it returns to Earth and lands vertically back on the launchpad.

Ready for refueling to take up another payload!

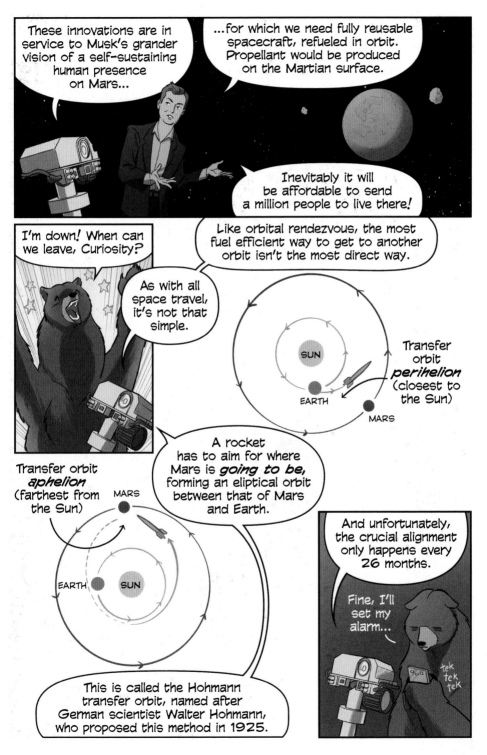

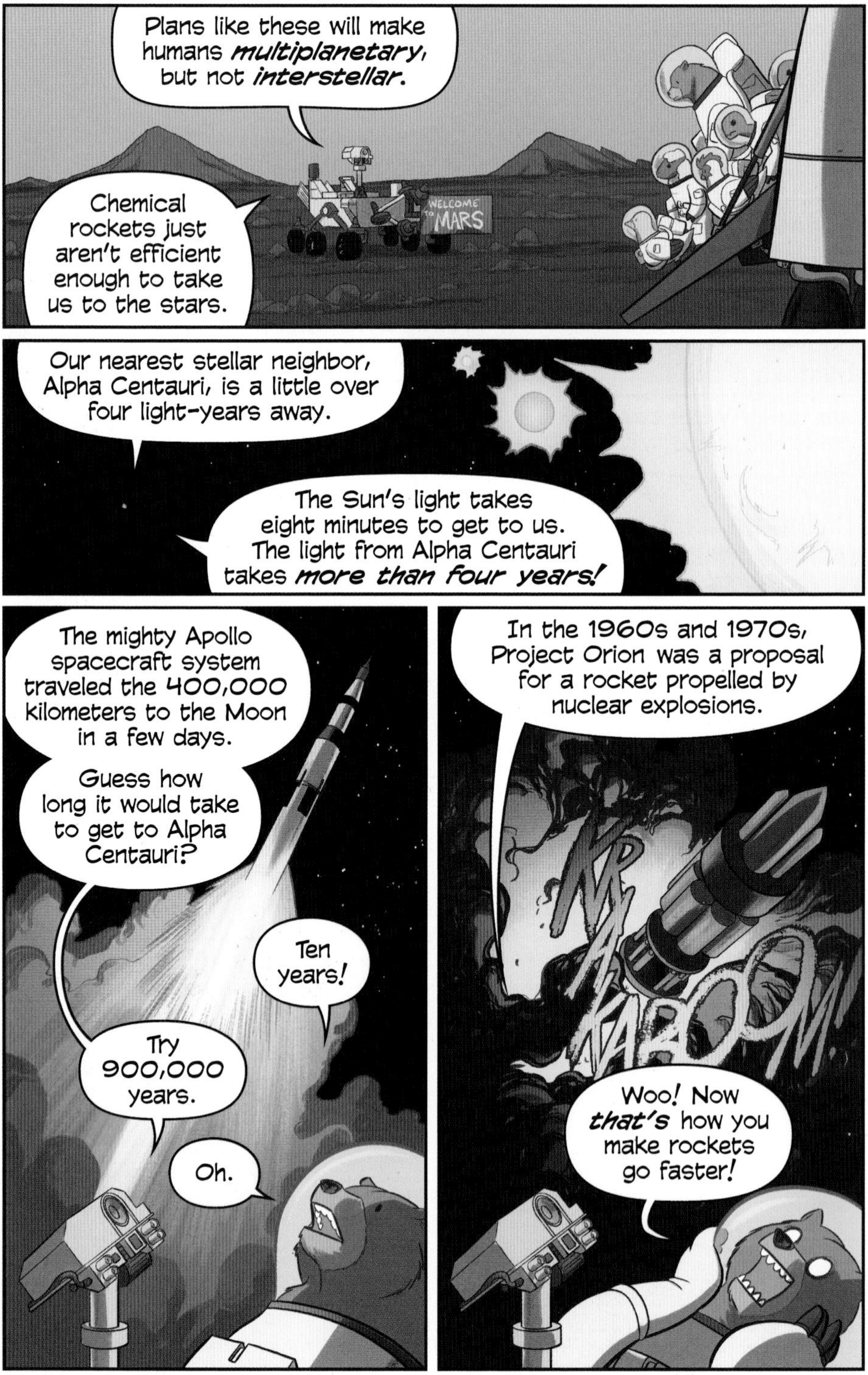

Plans like these will make humans *multiplanetary*, but not *interstellar*.
WELCOME TO MARS
Chemical rockets just aren't efficient enough to take us to the stars.
Our nearest stellar neighbor, Alpha Centauri, is a little over four light-years away.
The Sun's light takes eight minutes to get to us. The light from Alpha Centauri takes ***more than four years!***
The mighty Apollo spacecraft system traveled the 400,000 kilometers to the Moon in a few days.
Guess how long it would take to get to Alpha Centauri?
Ten years!
Try 900,000 years.
Oh.
In the 1960s and 1970s, Project Orion was a proposal for a rocket propelled by nuclear explosions.
KA KABOOM!
Woo! Now ***that's*** how you make rockets go faster!

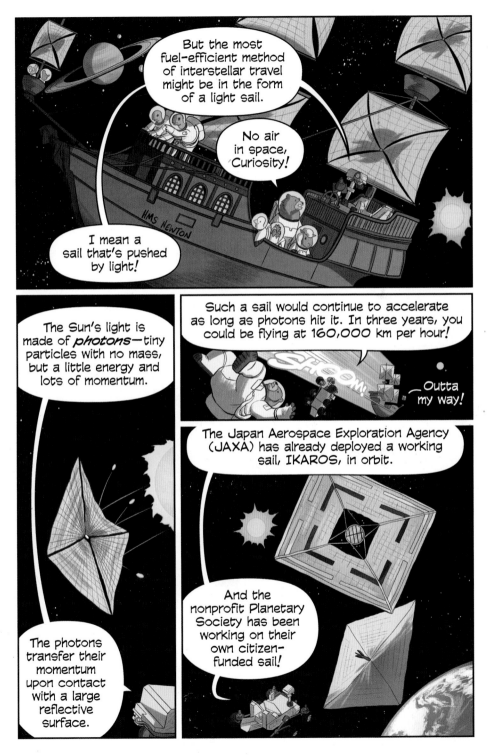

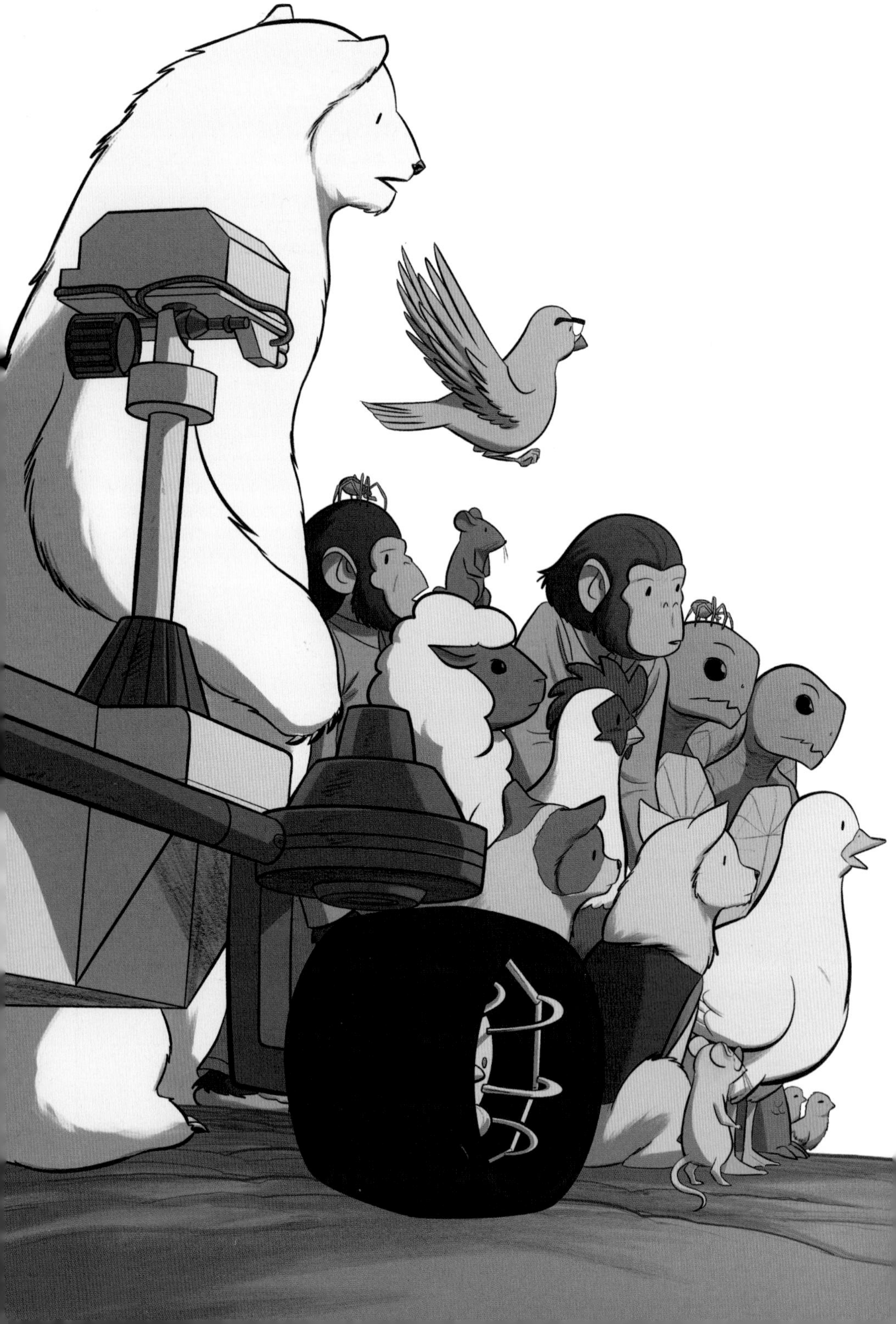

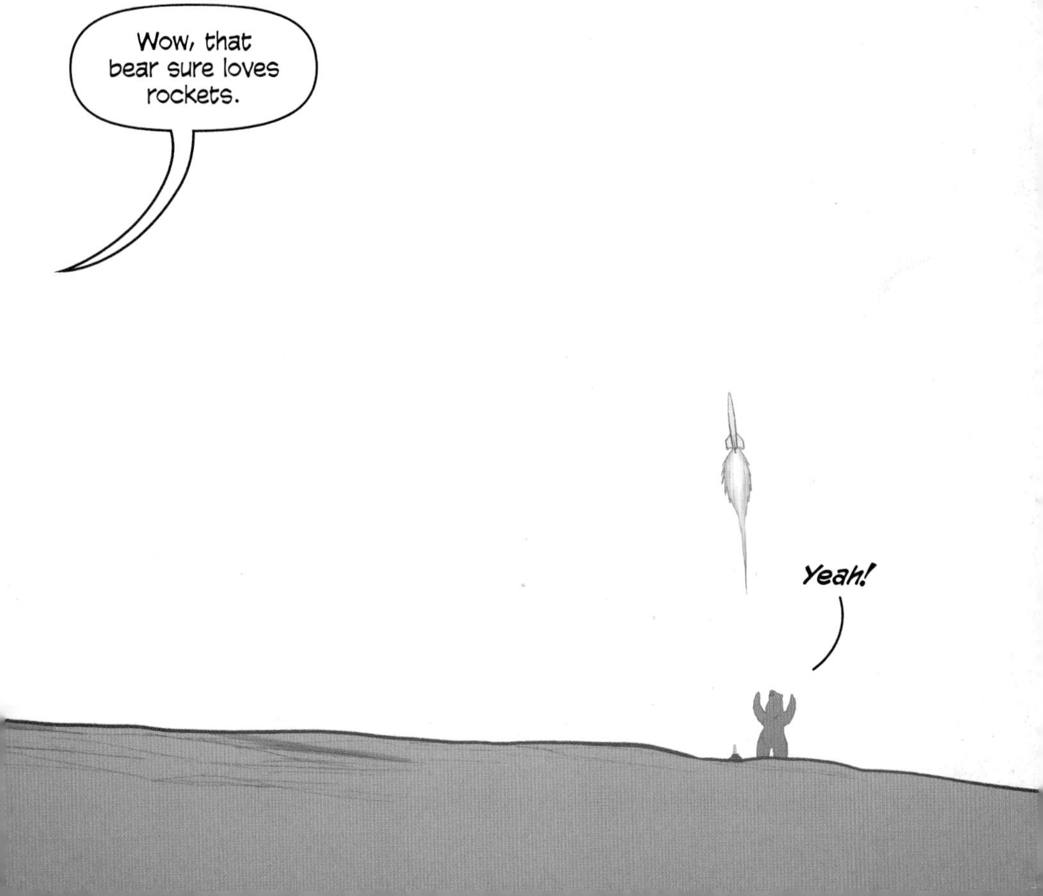
Wow, that bear sure loves rockets.
Yeah!

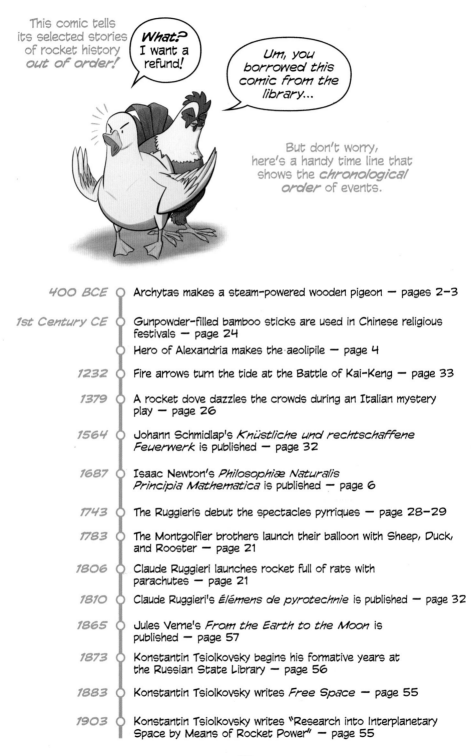

This comic tells its selected stories of rocket history ***out of order!***

What? I want a refund!
Um, you borrowed this comic from the library...

But don't worry, here's a handy time line that shows the ***chronological order*** of events.

400 BCE — Archytas makes a steam-powered wooden pigeon — pages 2–3

1st Century CE — Gunpowder-filled bamboo sticks are used in Chinese religious festivals — page 24

Hero of Alexandria makes the aeolipile — page 4

1232 — Fire arrows turn the tide at the Battle of Kai-Keng — page 33

1379 — A rocket dove dazzles the crowds during an Italian mystery play — page 26

1564 — Johann Schmidlap's *Knüstliche und rechtschaffene Feuerwerk* is published — page 32

1687 — Isaac Newton's *Philosophiæ Naturalis Principia Mathematica* is published — page 6

1743 — The Ruggieris debut the spectacles pyrriques — page 28–29

1783 — The Montgolfier brothers launch their balloon with Sheep, Duck, and Rooster — page 21

1806 — Claude Ruggieri launches rocket full of rats with parachutes — page 21

1810 — Claude Ruggieri's *Élémens de pyrotechnie* is published — page 32

1865 — Jules Verne's *From the Earth to the Moon* is published — page 57

1873 — Konstantin Tsiolkovsky begins his formative years at the Russian State Library — page 56

1883 — Konstantin Tsiolkovsky writes *Free Space* — page 55

1903 — Konstantin Tsiolkovsky writes "Research into Interplanetary Space by Means of Rocket Power" — page 55

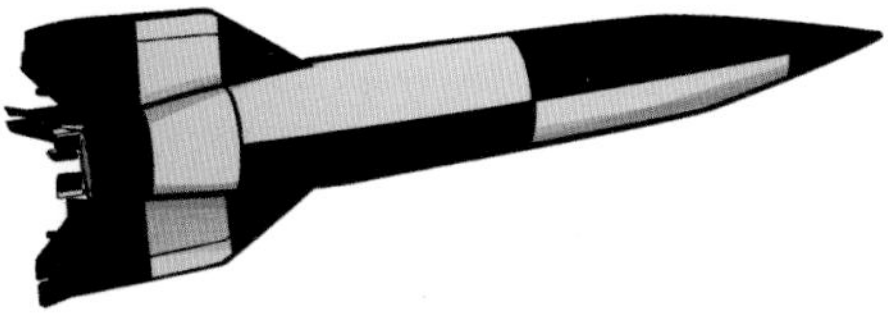

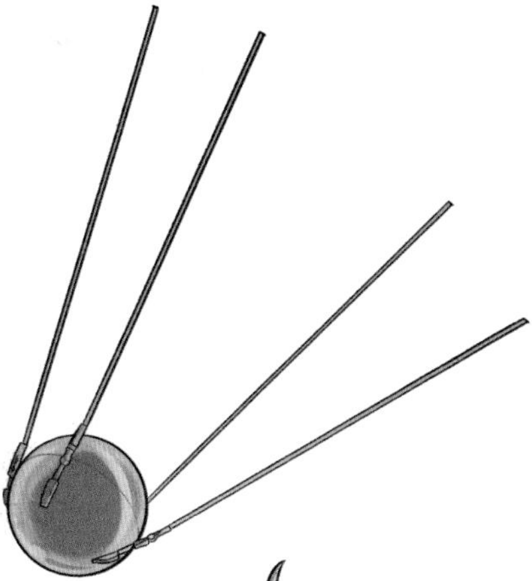

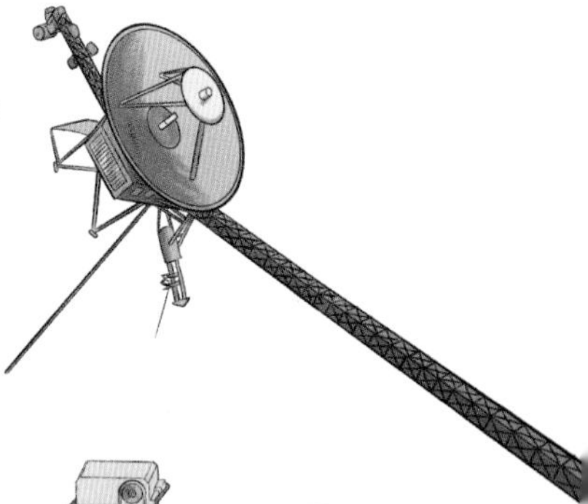

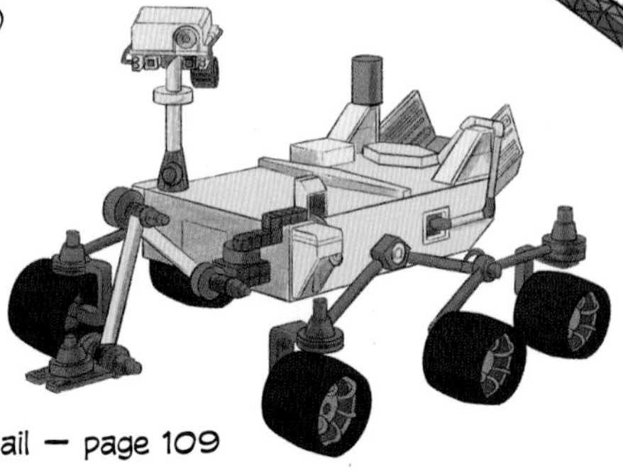

—GLOSSARY—

Acceleration — To change the speed of an object over time.

Center of mass (cm) — The point on an object where its mass is equally balanced on both sides.

Center of pressure (cp) — The point on an airborne object where the drag and lift forces acting on it are equal.

Center of thrust (cot) — The midpoint where thrust from a craft's reaction engines balances and the direction in which a craft's thrust is acting.

Drag — The resistance air exerts on a body moving through it.

Escape velocity — The velocity at which an object would escape the gravitational attraction of a given astronomical body. The escape velocity of the Earth is 11.2 kilometers per second.

Euthanize — To put to death without pain.

Exhaust velocity — The speed at which gas escapes from a rocket.

Fins — Fixed rudders on a rocket to help give it direction.

Flaps — Movable rudders, either attached to the fins or placed in the jet of a rocket, to direct the flight.

Force — A push or pull that changes the speed or direction of an object.

Friction — The resistance that one surface or object encounters when moving over another.

Fuel — The combustible component of a rocket propellant.

g (lowercase) — The symbol for gravity, the unit of acceleration, equal to 9.81 meters per second every second.

Gimbal — A pivoted support mechanism that allows attached objects to rotate around a central axis.

G-force — The force of gravity or acceleration on a body.

Gravity assist — The technique of using the energy of a gravitational field and the orbital velocity of a planet to change the speed and trajectory of a spacecraft.

Gyroscope — A device with a spinning disc used to stabilize, guide, or measure rotational movement.

Inertia — The tendency of matter to stay at rest or stay in motion unless acted upon by an outside force.

Initial mass — The mass of a rocket at the beginning of flight.

—GLOSSARY CONTINUED—

Initial velocity — The velocity of a rocket at the start of the firing period.

Mass — The amount of matter in an object.

Nozzle — A narrow opening at the base of a rocket that controls the flow of exhaust gases from its engine.

Orbit — The curved path an object or spacecraft around a star, planet, or moon.

Orientation — The determination of the relative position of something.

Oxidizer — A chemical needed by a fuel in order to burn. Most fuels use the oxygen in our atmosphere as their oxidizer, but a rocket must carry its own oxidizer when traveling into the vacuum of space.

Payload — The useful load carried by the rocket, in addition to its necessary structural weight and fuel.

Physics — The science of matter, motion, force, and energy.

Pitch — How a rocket is rotated on the y-axis. It describes whether the rocket's nose is up or down.

Propellant — A combination of fuel and oxidizer that burns to produce thrust in a rocket.

Rest — The state of an object when there are no unbalanced forces acting on it.

Rocket — An enclosed chamber with gas under pressure.

Roll — How a rocket is rotated on the x-axis. It describes the rotation of the rocket around an axis running from nose to tail.

Serial staging — A rocket consisting of several sections or "steps" fired successively, each step being jettisoned when its fuel is exhausted.

Space rendezvous — A series of orbital maneuvers to bring two spacecraft in close proximity.

Throat — The narrowest part of a rocket motor nozzle.

Thrust — The push produced by a jet or rocket motor.

Trajectory — The path followed by a projectile flying or an object moving under the action of given forces.

Vacuum — A space in which there is no air.

Yaw — How a rocket is rotated on the z-axis. It describes whether the nose is left or right.

—FURTHER READING—

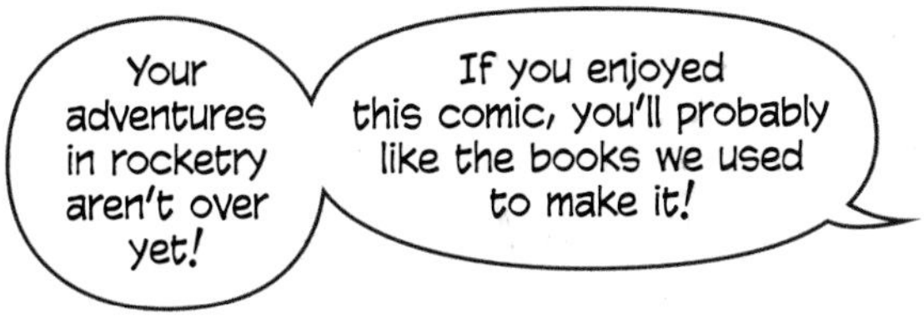
Your adventures in rocketry aren't over yet!
If you enjoyed this comic, you'll probably like the books we used to make it!

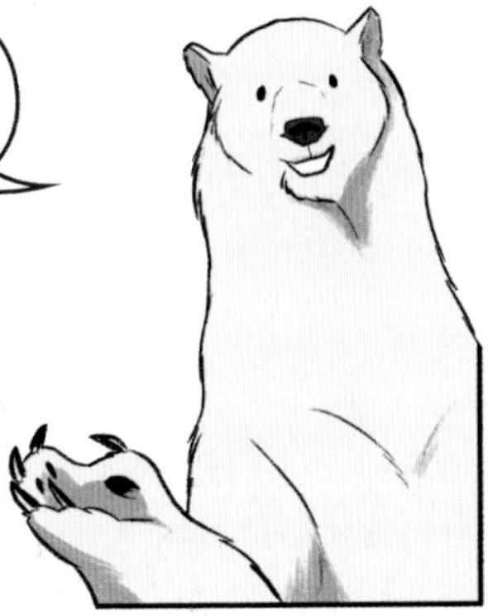

Gruntman, Mike. *Blazing the Trail: The Early History of Spacecraft and Rocketry*. American Institute of Aeronautics and Astronautics, 2004.

The History of Rocket Technology: Essays on Research, Development, and Utility, edited by Eugene M. Emme. Wayne State University Press, 1964.

Jet Propulsion: Journal of the American Rocket Society, v. 14–17. American Rocket Society, 1944–1947.

Morgan, George D. *Rocket Girl: The Story of Mary Sherman Morgan, America's First Female Rocket Scientist*. Prometheus Books, 2013.

Pyle, Rod. *Curiosity: An Inside Look at the Mars Rover Mission and the People Who Made It Happen*. Prometheus Books, 2014.

Rogers, Lucy. *It's ONLY Rocket Science: An Introduction in Plain English*. Springer, 2008.

Ryan, Craig. *Sonic Wind: The Story of John Paul Stapp and How a Renegade Doctor Became the Fastest Man on Earth*. W.W. Norton & Company, 2015.

Shetterly, Margot Lee. *Hidden Figures: The American Dream and the Untold Story of the Black Women Mathmeticians Who Helped Win the Space Race*. HarperCollins, 2016.

Vogt, Gregory L. *Rockets, information and activities for elementary teachers to use in preparing students for a unit on model rocketry*. NASA, 1992.

Werrett, Simon. *Fireworks: Pyrotechnic Arts & Sciences in European History*. The University of Chicago Press, 2010.

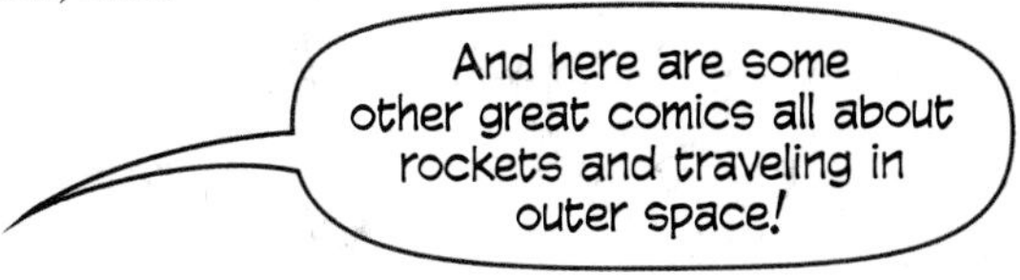
And here are some other great comics all about rockets and traveling in outer space!

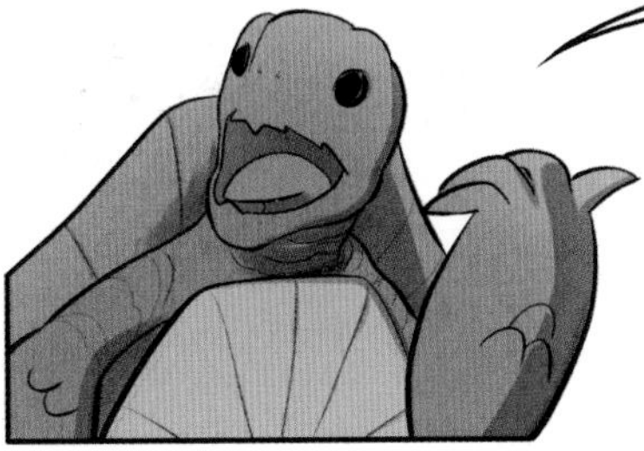

Abadzis, Nick. *Laika*. First Second Books, 2007.

Ottaviani, Jim, Zander Cannon, Kevin Cannon. *T-Minus: The Race to the Moon*. Alladin, 2009.